# Attention-Deficit/ Hyperactivity Disorder

*Other titles in* Diseases and People

—Diseases and People—

# Attention-Deficit/ Hyperactivity Disorder

Julie Williams

**Enslow Publishers, Inc.**

40 Industrial Road        PO Box 38
Box 398                 Aldershot
Berkeley Heights, NJ 07922    Hants GU12 6BP
USA                          UK
http://www.enslow.com

*For my children*

**Library of Congress Cataloging-in-Publication Data**

Williams, Julie, 1954-
    Attention-deficit/hyperactivity disorder / Julie Williams.
        p. cm. — (Diseases and people)
    Includes bibliographical references and index.
    ISBN 0-7660-1598-X
    1. Attention-deficit hyperactivity disorder—Juvenile literature.
    2. Attention-deficit-disordered children—Juvenile literature. 3. Hyperactive
children—Juvenile literature. [1. Attention-deficit hyperactivity disorder.]
    I. Title. II. Series.
    RJ506.H9 W55    2001
    618.92'8589—dc21                                           00-011931

Printed in the United States of America

10 9 8 7 6 5 4 3 2 1

**To Our Readers:**
We have done our best to make sure all Internet addresses in this book were active and appropriate when we went to press. However, the author and the publisher have no control over and assume no liability for the material available on those Internet sites or on other Web sites they may link to. Any comments or suggestions can be sent by e-mail to comments@enslow.com or to the address on the back cover.

**Photo Credits:** © Corel Corporation, pp.50, 83, 84, 87, 92, 95; Courtesy of the National Library of Medicine, pp. 34, 37; Díamar Interactive Corp., pp. 23, 61; Dover Publications, Inc., p.8; Enslow Publishers, Inc., p.20; Julie Williams, pp. 13, 30, 44, 74, 76; National Archives, p. 64, 99; University of California, Los Angeles, School of Medicine, p. 27.

**Cover Illustration:** Robert McCaw

# Contents

# ATTENTION-DEFICIT/ HYPERACTIVITY DISORDER (ADHD)

**What Is It?** A group of behaviors including, but not limited to:
Inattention—not paying attention when you really need to
Impulsivity—acting without thinking
Distractibility—getting off-track easily
Hyperactivity—inappropriate, excessive physical motions

**What Is The Correct Name?** Until 1994, this disorder was generally known as Attention Deficit Disorder (ADD). In 1994, the name officially changed to Attention-Deficit/Hyperactivity Disorder (ADHD), but many people still use the term ADD.

**Who Gets It?** ADHD is usually diagnosed in childhood. Behaviors often persist through adolescence into adulthood. It is more commonly identified in boys than girls, because of boys' tendency toward hyperactivity. All ethnic groups and economic classes are subject to ADHD. The highest number of cases reported is in the United States.

**How Do You Get It?** The cause of ADHD is unknown. It may be genetically passed from generation to generation. Research is being conducted to pinpoint causes, as well as to establish cures.

**What Are The Symptoms?** Inattention is a prime symptom. Impulsive behavior and getting distracted easily are also common. Hyperactivity appears frequently, especially in young children. These behaviors must occur for at least six months, be excessive, and occur in several different environments in order to qualify as ADHD.

**How Is It Treated?** A combination of some or all of: behavioral management, coaching, psychological therapy, social skills training, help at school, and medication. Schools are usually involved if the person with ADHD is a student.

**How Can It Be Prevented?** No one can answer this question at this time. Parent training and support for families with pre-school ADHD children may help lessen the symptoms as the children grow older.

Although Thomas Alva Edison lived before ADHD was identified, many people feel he had some of the characteristics, such as forgetfulness, impulsive behavior, and sudden bursts of intense activity.

# 1

# Not Just a Bratty Kid

**T**homas could never do well in school. One teacher called him "addled." His mother had to teach him at home. As an adult, he was constantly being fired from jobs. He moved frequently from house to house. One day he abruptly proposed to a young woman he had barely spoken to, and married her a week later. After the wedding ceremony, he went back to his office and forgot all about her until one of his co-workers reminded him that he now had a wife!

Thomas Alva Edison lived before Attention-Deficit/Hyperactivity Disorder was identified, but many people feel he had some of its characteristics, such as forgetfulness, impulsive behavior, and sudden bursts of intense activity. Edison frequently made his workers stay on the job with him for several days without sleep or food, when he felt the project was important. Despite his unpredictable behavior, he was able to invent the electric light bulb, the phonograph, and moving pictures. He made improvements to many machines and devices still used today.[1]

The ability to think before acting and to control one's behavior grows as a person matures. Young children are usually very active and likely to rush into something. When Edison did not develop the self-control his teachers expected, his mother's only choice was to teach him at home. Today, if a child shows this same kind of impulsive or distracted behavior, the child's parents or teachers may consider evaluating the child to see if he or she has Attention-Deficit/Hyperactivity Disorder. This term, usually abbreviated ADHD, covers a wide spectrum of behaviors including acting impulsively, being easily distracted, not paying attention, and excessive, inappropriate physical activity. An older term, Attention Deficit Disorder (ADD), is sometimes still used.

Everyone gets distracted sometimes. Everyone forgets things now and then. Everyone gets excited and acts without thinking occasionally. These actions are all part of normal behavior. ADHD is suspected when these types of behavior occur very frequently, or in a way that interferes with a person's ability to function at school, home, or work.

Some people with ADHD are overactive. Others seem dreamy and forgetful. Some, like Edison, are both. There are different subtypes of ADHD.

ADHD affects over two million school-aged children in the United States, and an unknown number of adults.[2] One estimate claims that five million children and adults have sought treatment for ADHD.[3] ADHD begins in childhood, but recently people have become aware that ADHD often continues into adulthood. It can be a lifetime condition, and does not always go away when a person reaches maturity.

Six to eight times as many boys as girls are diagnosed with ADHD, probably because boys are more physically active and get noticed more frequently. People with ADHD may have other conditions, such as learning disabilities or depression. Their intellectual ability is usually in the normal range.

Despite the large number of people who exhibit ADHD behaviors, there is no known cause or cure. Current research has identified chemical imbalances in the brain that may be associated with ADHD. There may also be structural abnormalities in the brain itself. Family, school, and community environments may have an effect on the severity of ADHD symptoms, but they are not the cause of the disorder.

Changes in a person's environment, behavioral and psychological counseling, and changes in diet can help lessen the effect of ADHD. Different kinds of medications may help lessen the symptoms in some people. No known medication cures ADHD, however, and the use of medication to treat ADHD is controversial. One psychologist whose children were diagnosed with ADHD and received medication feels that "Ritalin [a stimulant medication commonly prescribed for ADHD] is not a drug to be trifled with. It is an amphetamine...And yet each year Ritalin—or some related drug—is being prescribed for millions of children as a quick fix for not

# What Is an IQ Test, Anyway?

The term Intelligence Quotient (IQ) was coined in 1916 by the American psychologist Lewis M. Terman. It attempts to describe a person's ability to understand, learn, and think. The IQ, always expressed as a number, is the result of dividing a person's score on an intelligence test by the person's actual age. For example, a seven year old with a test score of eight has an IQ of 8 divided by 7, or 114. (The actual result is 1.14, but since the decimal serves no useful function it is just left out.)

Tests used to determine intellectual ability originated in the 1800s. Sir Francis Galton, a cousin of the famous evolutionist Charles Darwin, was the first to try to measure the human intellect in precise terms. His tests did not provide reliable results, however. In 1905, the French psychologist Alfred Binet developed questions that measured a person's ability to identify patterns, draw analogies, and form judgments. One part of his test consisted of incomplete sentences, for which the person being tested had to supply missing words. This type of question is still used today.

Binet's original test questions have been adapted over the years, and form part of the Stanford-Binet IQ test, which is still in use today. The two tests most commonly employed today are the Wechsler Adult Intelligence Scale (WAIS) and the Wechsler Intelligence Scale for Children (WISC). Questions on these tests focus on how quickly a person organizes and remembers information, his or her general memory and attention to detail, visual alertness, vocabulary, and knowledge of arithmetic.[4]

behaving well or for not doing their schoolwork with care."[5] A pediatric specialist at Massachusetts General Hospital in Boston takes a completely opposite view. He feels that "the sharp rise in the use of Ritalin can be seen as negative or positive. I see it as positive. Treatment rates are catching up to diagnosis rates."[6]

Most instances of ADHD are discovered when a child goes to school. This means that the schools play a major role in identifying and treating ADHD. The diagnosis of ADHD results from a complex battery of physical, educational, and psychological assessments. Effective treatment requires a team

In most schools, children are expected to sit quietly and learn through low-stimulation methods, such as group lectures and individual worksheets.

# Three Types of Attention-Deficit/Hyperactivity Disorder[7]

ADHD—predominantly inattentive

ADHD—predominantly hyperactive-impulsive

ADHD—combined inattentive and hyperactive-impulsive

approach involving doctors, psychologists, learning specialists, teachers, and the family.

Interestingly, the United States has a much higher incidence of ADHD than other countries. Researchers disagree on whether it is underdiagnosed in other countries, or overdiagnosed in the U.S. In Europe, for example, ADHD symptoms must occur in every aspect of a person's life for a doctor to make a diagnosis of ADHD, not just in two situations, as in the U.S.[8] Because of this fact, and because experts do not always agree on a definition of ADHD, some people feel that ADHD is not a true medical disorder. They point out that American children grow up in a high-stimulation environment of short sound bites, graphic video games, and instant e-messaging. Yet in school they are expected to sit quietly and learn through low-stimulation methods such as group lectures and individual worksheets. Adults, too, are accustomed to instant responses from cell phones, fax machines, and palm pilots.

Is it surprising that the rate of adult ADHD is growing faster than in any other group?

Researchers are making tremendous progress in understanding how the brain works. We are also learning how our environment influences our biological inheritance, or genetics. In the case of ADHD, both biology and environment play crucial roles.

# 2

# What Is ADHD?

Fourteen-year-old Jasper rearranged his textbooks on his desk for the tenth time. He drummed his fingers to the beat of his favorite song playing in his head, louder and louder until the other kids around him stopped laughing and started frowning. When the teacher asked him a question, he could not seem to spit the answer out quickly, even though he knew it. So he made a wisecrack instead, and received an instant trip to the principal's office. Gym was his favorite class—the coach did not get mad when he gave a little extra shove in soccer practice. The other boys did, though. He did not have a lot of friends. But in spite of his behavior, he always did pretty well in school.

At home, things were not much better. Jasper and his brother fought all the time. His parents thought he could be doing a lot better in school. Jasper thought so too, but he was not about to tell his parents how frustrated he felt. They took him to a counselor once. It did not help.

Nan was eight. She got along pretty well with her brother and sister, and had some friends at school. In class she sat quietly and did not participate much. She was an average student, and had never been a behavior problem. But this year, when she turned her first math test in, she got only two problems right out of thirty. Her teacher was shocked. So was Nan!

Both Jasper and Nan are going to be evaluated for Attention-Deficit/Hyperactivity Disorder. ADHD is an umbrella term used to describe a constant, serious lack of self-controlled behavior in situations such as school, work, and home. In order to qualify as ADHD, this lack of control cannot just be annoying to other people. It must be causing problems for the person who has it. For example, if Jasper let off steam by making rude remarks about people when he was alone, it would not be a serious problem. Smarting off to a teacher, however, is serious.

Some people experience a combination of these problem behaviors, others only a few. The behavior may be mild, like dropping your bookbag because you are staring at leaves waving in the wind. It may be very intense, like screaming at your mom because she is five minutes late picking you up from school. Sometimes a new or changed situation will push a person's self-control to the edge, and allow the negative behaviors to become stronger. Feeling stressed can step up the problems.[1]

# Core Behaviors

Several types of behavior are considered typical, or core, aspects of ADHD.[2] Others are less typical, but still form part of the wide range of difficulties with self-control.

# Inattention/Distractibility

Nan loved watching the sunlight come through the miniblinds in the kitchen at home. Her mother was talking to her, but she was so focused on the light dancing on the wall that she did not hear what her mom said. When lunchtime came around, Nan realized she did not have her lunchbox with her. Her mother had been trying to tell her where she had put the lunch box, but Nan wasn't listening.

Jasper did not want to pay attention to his teachers. He wanted to join the Air Force and fly jets as soon as he graduated from high school. What did French history have to do with that? He wanted to be moving, going places, doing things! Since he lacked interest, he did not tune in when the teacher gave the class their homework assignment.

Nan and Jasper were both paying attention, but not to what they were supposed to be paying attention to. They were easily distracted by something else, whether it was something pretty on the wall, or a fantasy about the future. This distracted behavior caused both children big problems.

# Impulsivity

When Jasper got mad, everyone ran. He usually threw something. Once in a while, he slugged somebody. Whenever something went wrong he lashed out. He could not seem to control himself. Afterward, he felt bad, especially when no one would hang around with him.

Nan always had trouble choosing clothes when she went shopping. All the different choices, the people walking around, and the noise in the stores made it hard for her to think clearly about what she needed. She would quickly pick out a lot of clothes just so she could get out of the store. When she got home she would realize she could not wear most of what she had chosen. Her mother started ordering from a catalogue because she did not have the time to spend driving back and forth to the mall exchanging Nan's clothes. Nan disliked most of her clothes, but could not endure the noise and confusion of shopping long enough to pick clothes that she would actually wear.

Impulsivity is acting without thinking of the consequences. Both Jasper and Nan share this trait.

## Hyperactivity

Hyperactivity, or excessive, inappropriate physical activity, is the best known symptom of ADHD, probably because it is the most noticeable. It varies in intensity from person to person. Excessive activity is usually highest in small children, and boys are often more hyperactive than girls.

Hyperactivity does not refer to the normal fantastic energy that most small children have. It refers to excessive, inappropriate motion, as if a person were driven by a motor running inside that does not shut off. As a small boy, Jasper was a

ADHD children have problems with all the different choices a mall has to offer.

human tornado. As an adolescent he was still restless, constantly tapping his fingers and shifting from foot to foot, but he had matured enough to be able to sit in a chair for most of a class period.

Some people move from one activity to another without finishing any of them. Other people cannot stop talking. These are also instances of hyperactivity.

Not everyone with attention difficulties is hyperactive. For instance, Nan was always calm, even as a little girl.

## Other Behaviors Associated With ADHD

Both Nan and Jasper had trouble organizing and completing their schoolwork. By the time they finished their homework at night, they, and their parents, were exhausted.

Sometimes, however, they would bring home a ton of homework and polish it off in a few minutes. In reality, the homework was no easier than it usually was, but for some unknown reason they were able to focus on it. This is called a "variable response" to a specific situation.

Difficulty in getting along with other people, due to not paying attention to others and reacting without thinking, is common.

A low tolerance for frustration, getting angry easily, and temper tantrums are also seen. Not following rules and instructions may be a problem.

Some people with ADHD can be very stubborn. They keep trying to do things in a way that does not work. They do not learn from experience. This is called perseveration.

A few people with ADHD have an insatiable need for attention. They might be daredevils, trying stunts that are reckless and dangerous.[3]

## Doesn't Everyone Act Like That?

Of course, at times everyone zones out, or acts impulsively, or runs around. Babies cry the moment they are hungry or want something, even in the middle of a wedding! No one expects a baby to understand when it is okay to make noise and when it is not okay. As babies mature, however, people expect them to control their impulses and pay attention more and more. When this self-control has not developed in an age-appropriate way, there may be a developmental delay. A developmental delay is a disruption in a person's expected growth pattern. The delay may be temporary or long lasting. ADHD is one type of developmental disorder.

## A Controversial Definition

No one definition of ADHD is accepted by everyone. However, when talking about and working with ADHD, most doctors, psychologists, and teachers make a few basic assumptions:

- ADHD is a developmental disorder.

- ADHD is a behavioral disorder, meaning it is identified by a person's actions. ADHD behaviors have in common a lack of self-control or self-regulation. It is not possible to identify

Babies lack self-control. As babies mature, people expect them to control their impulses and pay attention more and more.

ADHD by what a person looks like, or how he or she acts in just one situation at one time.

- There is no single test, or series of tests, that identifies ADHD with total certainty. No blood test, chromosome analysis, or score on an exam can reveal ADHD.[4]

- All diagnoses of ADHD are subjective. This means that the identification and interpretation of the behaviors depends on the point of view of the observer. Some observers are more likely to feel that certain behaviors indicate ADHD than others.

23

# The Basis of ADHD

Researchers are trying to discover the threads that bind the different ADHD behaviors together. One basic characteristic, the lack of self-control, seems to underlie them all. The technical term for this condition is *behavioral disinhibition,* meaning the inability to plan, control, and regulate one's own behavior.[5] For example, Jasper was home one afternoon studying for a big biology test when one of his few friends called. He had a ride to the mall and wanted to go play video games and hang out. Jasper really wanted to pass the test, but the test was tomorrow and the mall was right now. He told himself he would study when he got home and closed his book. The more important goal of passing the test got lost because he found something more fun and immediate to do.

The inability to control one's own behavior can arise often, in many different situations. Someone feels like talking out loud in a movie and does. People daydream instead of paying attention in traffic, or rush out of the house without checking to see if all the doors are locked. All of these actions can have negative consequences. But they do not add up to ADHD until they happen much more frequently and cause more problems than in most other people at the same stage of development.

# Who Has ADHD?

Given the difficulty of defining ADHD, determining the number of people who have it is also difficult. Children,

24

adolescents, and adults can all have ADHD. We do know that it is the most commonly diagnosed behavioral disorder in children.[6] Most estimates say that 3–6 percent of school-aged children show some signs of ADHD.[7] Over 2 million school-aged children have been identified with ADHD behaviors.[8] One researcher claims that up to 10 percent of American children show significant ADHD symptoms.[9]

Until recently, it was thought that children with ADHD outgrew it by the time they became adults. Research now shows that up to two-thirds of people with ADHD as children will still have some ADHD symptoms as adults.[10] Up to 25 percent of the people taking medication for ADHD symptoms are adults.

The incidence of ADHD is not limited to any one group of people or any one geographical area. Because it is expensive to diagnose, people with lower incomes may not be identified and receive help. The United States accounts for almost all the worldwide cases of ADHD, and uses most of the medications prescribed for ADHD.

Boys exhibit more hyperactive, aggressive, and acting-out types of behavior than girls do. This means they are much more likely than girls to be evaluated and diagnosed with ADHD. Estimates of the ratio of ADHD in boys versus girls run from 8-to-1 to 3-to-1.[11] Most experts feel that girls are underidentified, and that the incidence of ADHD is about equal in both sexes. Girls tend to keep their problems inside and so suffer from higher rates of depression, underachievement, and social isolation.[12]

# Causes

Since there is no test for ADHD, unlike a disease such as diabetes, pinpointing its causes is difficult. Little is known about possible prenatal causes of ADHD. Brain injuries caused by accidents or infections and disorders in brain development account for a very small percentage of ADHD cases. Exposure to lead from old paint and a mother's use of drugs and alcohol while pregnant contribute a few cases.[13]

Almost everyone agrees that ADHD behaviors arise from many different sources. Two major areas being studied are the brain and a person's surroundings, or environment.

# The Brain

In 1990, Dr. Alan Zametkin at the National Institute of Mental Health in Washington, D.C., created a stir when he suggested that certain parts of the brains of people with ADHD might be less active than the brains of people without ADHD.[14]

Dr. Zametkin reached this conclusion by taking pictures of people's brains while they were thinking. He injected a radioactive substance into one of his subject's arteries, then asked the person to concentrate, and took pictures of the substance as it flowed into the brain. He used a technique called Positron Emission Tomography, or PET scanning, to take pictures of the part of the brain thought to control attention. These areas include the frontal and prefrontal cortexes, and the basal ganglia. He found a decreased blood flow in those areas in the people he was studying, compared to people who did not have ADHD.

The original study was conducted on parents of children who had been identified with ADHD and who exhibited some symptoms of ADHD themselves. No one would inject a radioactive material into the brain of a child. Thus, the study was not actually conducted on people with ADHD. A later study by Dr. Zametkin on adolescents with ADHD did not firmly support his original findings.[15] However, they point the way for further research.

Scientists have been able to study the size and shape of the different parts of the brain using another sophisticated technique, Magnetic Resonance Imaging, or MRI. MRI uses a magnet to take pictures of soft tissues inside a person's body.

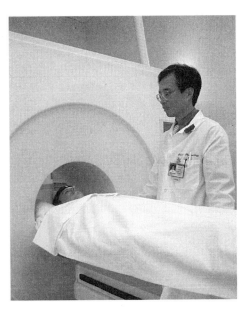

Positron Emission Tomography, or PET scanning, can be used to take pictures of the part of the brain thought to control attention.

MRI works very well on the brain. A new version of this technique, called functional MRI (fMRI), can show the brain and other organs as they work, much like the PET scan, and does not use radioactive material.

MRI and fMRI studies on people with ADHD symptoms suggest that slight differences in brain anatomy may, in fact, exist. However, the studies have looked at very small groups of subjects, and the results are not at all certain.[16]

## Chemicals in the Brain

Other brain research is looking at the role of special chemicals in the brain. These chemicals, called neurotransmitters, help information to pass from cell to cell in the brain. Two chemicals in particular, dopamine and norepinephrine, seem to be in short supply in the brains of people with ADHD. Research shows that when these chemicals are low or not available in areas of the brain associated with attention, the brain does not quiet down enough to allow a person to pay attention to something important. The brain is too "noisy" to pay attention.[17]

Imagine sitting in a large airport lounge. You are waiting for your best friend, whom you have not seen in a long time. Loud, bland music pours out of invisible speakers. The couple next to you is having a fight. Suddenly, two arrival gates open and streams of people pour into the lounge. Laughter and tears, flowers and gifts surround you. People are everywhere. You do not see your friend until she is suddenly standing right in front of you, laughing because you did not see her first. This is what a "noisy" brain is like.

## The Genetic Connection

A tendency toward ADHD behavior may be inherited. A study of identical twins, children born from a single egg that has divided, showed a 59 percent chance that both would have ADHD behavior if one had it. Fraternal twins, twins born of two eggs fertilized separately, were only 33 percent likely to have ADHD behavior if one had it. Brothers, sisters, and parents of a person with ADHD are more likely to have ADHD than the relatives of a person who does not have ADHD. Researchers are trying to determine what, if anything, is being passed along.[18]

## Environment

Biology provides only one piece of the puzzle of ADHD. Environmental factors play an equally large role. Environmental factors are any influences outside the brain itself. These include the family, school, and community, as well as a person's own actions. It is possible that a person's biological makeup provides the starting point for the core features of ADHD. However, the environment strongly influences how frequently and severely the behaviors appear.

The family, particularly parent-child relationships, plays a crucial role in shaping a person's behavior. Positive, nurturing

A structured, supportive environment at school can reduce learning problems faced by a student with ADHD.

interaction and attention from parents teach a child to interact positively with others.[19] As a child gets older, school has a major effect. A structured, supportive environment in school can reduce learning problems faced by a student with ADHD and increase the likelihood of academic success.[20] For adults, the careful choice of a career and small adjustments in the work situation can spell the difference between failure and success.[21]

# 3

# The History of ADHD

**A**DHD has been recognized as a distinct disorder only since 1902. But references to overactive, inattentive, and distracted behavior appear in medical writings over the past twenty-five hundred years. Some of the descriptions and treatments sound remarkably up-to-date.

The ancient Greeks thought that four bodily humors, or fluids, combined in the body to determine a person's health and personality. Too much black bile in a person's system, for instance, makes a person sad. Too much yellow bile makes a person get angry quickly.[1] Doctors today do not believe in the theory of humors. However, researchers today believe that many of our basic personality traits, such as being happy or depressed, lively or quiet, have their origins in the biochemical makeup of our brains.[2]

31

The Greeks also believed that energy, which they called "innate heat," is greatest in young people, and that it declines with age. Modern doctors have observed that hyperactivity, one component of ADHD, is greatest in young children, and decreases as a person grows up.

The key to treating an illness, according to ancient Greek theory, is cooperation among the physician, patient, and attendants. Circumstances, or a person's environment, must also be favorable for recovery.[3] Present-day strategies for treating ADHD stress the inclusion of the physical, educational, social, and family dimensions of a person's life.

In the Middle Ages, medical writers identified a type of behavior they called "frenzy." Some of these "frenzied" people might have been what we call hyperactive. At this time, frenzy was thought to be caused by demons possessing one's body, or by divine punishment for having done something wrong. As is still the case today, physicians disagreed over treatment. Drugs, letting out "excess" blood, or throwing people into rivers as a form of shock treatment were all tried. People could be locked up or even executed for being "different." A woman might be accused of being a witch and be burned at the stake.[4]

Bartholomew Anglicus, an English Franciscan monk of the twelfth century, had some suggestions for treatment of frenzy. A frenzied person, whom he defined as someone who is seldom still but cries much, should eat a few wet bread crumbs, and no more. His head must first be shaved and washed in lukewarm vinegar, then wrapped in pig's lungs. After that, the person's temples must be washed with lettuce juice. The vein in the forehead should be bled, enough to fill an eggshell. Everyone around him must be quiet, and he must not look at any pictures, especially pictures of people. If the person was not cured in three days, no recovery was possible.[5]

In the early 1600s, during the Renaissance, a Swiss doctor named Felix Platter wrote two books about psychiatric disorders. Although he could not deny the existence of demons, for fear of being executed for heresy, he downplayed their power to cause difficult behavior. Instead, he advised physical, psychological, and drug therapies for his patients.[6] Some of the calming drugs used at the time were poppies, henbane, and mandrake.[7]

Modern understanding of the brain as the source of behavior and feelings began with the great French philosopher, René Descartes (1596-1650). He said that human beings are composed of two parts, the body and the soul. He described the soul, which is the seat of human consciousness, as immortal and perfect. According to Descartes, the soul cannot be responsible for mental problems. Therefore, the workings of the mind must be determined by the physical matter of the brain.[8]

Following Descartes, doctors of his time attempted to map specific mental activities onto specific parts of the brain. These mapping efforts continue to this day, using sophisticated imaging techniques such as Magnetic Resonance Imaging (MRI) and Computerized Axial Tomography (CAT).

The nineteenth century saw an explosion in the study of the human mind and human behavior. Dr. Sigmund Freud

The great French philosopher, René Descartes, said that human beings are composed of two parts, the body and the soul. He described the soul, which is the seat of human consciousness, as immortal and perfect. According to Descartes, the soul cannot be responsible for mental problems. There, the workings of the mind must be determined by the physical matter of the brain.

(1856-1939), the founder of modern psychology, taught that people's behavior was rooted in the way they had been treated as children by their parents, particularly their mothers. Although this view caused many parents a lot of unnecessary guilt, it did make people aware of the powerful effect of the family and environment on a person's behavior.

## Philip's Behavior

Dr. Heinrich Hoffman was a very successful pediatrician and psychiatrist in Frankfurt, Germany. He is best known, however, as a writer of children's books which he published between 1845 and 1871. In his first book, called *Pleasant Stories and Funny Pictures,* he told in poetry the story of a "naughty, restless child" called Philip. Philip wriggles and giggles and nightly tilts his chair at the dinner table until he pulls the tablecloth and all the dishes down onto the floor. Dr. Hoffman did not give Philip's behavior a name, but this poem marks the first literary appearance of ADHD.[9]

## The Evolution of a Name

In 1902, Dr. George Still of England identified a distinct class of behavior in children which he called "volitional inhibition." Excessive inappropriate activity, poor attention span, and academic and behavior problems were its main features. Dr. Still considered these actions to indicate moral defects in children's ability to control their actions and to follow rules of social conduct. He thought the cause lay in the

35

brain, although he did not rule out influences from family and surroundings.

A few years later, researchers began to look for possible causes of these behaviors. Following the lead of Dr. Still, they looked to the brain for answers. At first, terms such as "restlessness syndrome" and "organic drivenness" were used, because the hyperactive behavior overshadowed all other aspects. A major outbreak of encephalitis, an inflammation of the brain, occurred in the United States in 1917–1918. Doctors and nurses who cared for infected children noticed a change in their behavior after the inflammation went down. They became restless and had trouble concentrating and controlling their impulses. This behavior was so similar to children with "organic drivenness" that doctors decided the cause of all restless behavior must be some kind of brain injury. The name of the disorder was changed to "brain-injured child syndrome."

In the 1950s, it became apparent that children who had not suffered any kind of brain injury could also be restless and hyperactive. The diagnostic term then changed to "minimal brain damage" or "minimal brain dysfunction."

The focus of research shifted away from the brain to the environment in the 1960s. As in the days of Sigmund Freud, parents, especially mothers, were blamed for the child's problems. It was at this time that the American Psychiatric Association (APA), a national organization of doctors specializing in psychology and psychiatry, first created an official diagnostic category for this behavior, Hyperkinetic Reaction of

In 1902, Dr. George Still of England identified a distinct class of behavior in children which he called "volitional inhibition."

Childhood, in the second edition of their standard reference work, *Diagnostic and Statistical Manual of Mental Disorders*.[10]

In 1972, Dr. Virginia Douglas of Canada recognized that the frantic activity of many children was concealing something else: difficulty controlling impulses and paying attention. As a result of the work by Dr. Douglas and others, the APA created two new diagnostic categories in 1980. The first category, Attention Deficit Disorder (ADD—an abbreviation still often used), was limited to inattention and distractibility. The second, Attention Deficit Disorder with Hyperactivity (ADD-H), included the first two behaviors and added impulsive and excessive activity.

These new categories reflected a fundamental change in the understanding of this disorder. Inattention, not hyperactivity, became its chief defining characteristic. This change in focus widened the group eligible for such a diagnosis. Not all people who have trouble paying attention are also hyperactive. Many of the people now eligible for an ADD diagnosis were girls, who are not usually as overactive as boys, and adults, most of whom have outgrown the hyperactivity aspect of this condition.[11]

The APA revised the names of the diagnostic categories slightly in 1987. ADD became Undifferentiated Attention Deficit Disorder, and ADD-H was renamed Attention-Deficit/Hyperactivity Disorder.

The year 1994 saw another change in the categories, to the terminology used today. Now there is only one category, Attention-Deficit/Hyperactivity Disorder, but it is divided into three subtypes: inattentive, hyperactive, and combined, including both inattentive and hyperactive.

These frequent name changes indicate that our understanding of this group of behaviors is not complete. As our knowledge grows, we can expect both the name and the definition to continue to change.

## The Origin of Treatments for ADHD

Dr. William Bradley worked at the Emma Pendleton Bradley Home for Children in Providence, Rhode Island. Children at the Bradley Home suffered from a wide variety of neurological, meaning brain-based, and behavioral disorders. As part of a complete diagnosis for such illnesses, many of the children had to have spinal taps. In a spinal tap, the fluid surrounding the spinal cord is extracted with a needle for testing. A common aftereffect of a spinal tap is a severe headache.

In 1937, Dr. Bradley was trying to find a way to ease the headaches the children experienced after having spinal taps.[12] He tried giving the children a medication called Benzedrine for their headaches. Benzedrine is a combination of two different stimulant medications. He was surprised to find that in addition to helping with the headaches, it seemed to calm the children down. He also noticed that the children did better at their schoolwork while taking the medication, and obeyed the staff's directions much more readily. He was surprised because, like most other doctors, he theorized that a stimulant would make the children more active and less likely to concentrate on homework and do what they were asked.[13]

No one believed that stimulants could actually calm someone down when Dr. Bradley published the results of his experiences. Slowly, doctors began to accept Bradley's findings, but they still believed that stimulants worked to control ADHD only on children. Eventually, controlled, scientific trials of stimulants as a treatment for children with attention deficit and hyperactivity were conducted in the early 1960s. Many of the children in the trials showed improvement in impulse control, attention, and lowered activity levels. Later research has shown that stimulants work by helping people of all ages improve their focus. Their effect is not limited to children.

At this time another stimulant, Ritalin, was developed specifically for ADHD. Ritalin was approved for treatment of ADHD in children by the Food and Drug Administration in 1961.

# 4
# Identifying ADHD in Children and Adults

**N**an sat outside the school counselor's office. Her palms felt clammy. She did not know exactly why she was there. Yesterday she had visited her family doctor, who had asked a lot of questions. Now she was here.

Mrs. Smith opened the door and smiled. "Hello, Nan," she said. "I've got a few tests for you to complete. They're very short. Don't worry."

Nan was in the midst of a comprehensive evaluation. This is the name given to the tests required by law to establish causes and determine corrective action when a student exhibits serious academic difficulties in school. Her teacher, Mrs. Hunter, felt her school work was lagging behind that of the other children in her class. Mrs. Hunter had many years of teaching experience and had recently attended a teacher training seminar on ADHD. She knew Nan needed help, and knew how to get the process started to get it.

Mrs. Hunter's first call was to Nan's parents. They were surprised and upset to hear that their daughter was having trouble in school, but they were eager to find a way for her to get help. They met with Nan's teacher and counselor to discuss the process. At the end of the meeting, they gave their consent to a comprehensive evaluation to screen for learning disabilities and ADHD. After the tests are completed, they will all meet again to decide if Nan has a form of ADHD and/or other learning problems. Then they will decide what to do about it.

Schools are required by law to look for students who are having academic trouble and to evaluate and help them. This is called the "child find" obligation.[1] If Nan's parents had not agreed to allow her to be tested, the law provides a procedure to allow the school to evaluate and help her, even without her parents' consent.

## ADHD in the School Setting

ADHD is often identified when a child begins formal education. It usually shows up in the first three years of school. The child is probably behaving the same way as he or she does at home and did in preschool, but now the school environment is more demanding. Even kindergarten requires children to follow rules and pay attention.[2]

However, not all kids are identified early. Jasper managed to get by on his intelligence, which was well above average, until he hit adolescence. His behavior had never been perfect.

But all the changes taking place in his body and his intensifying emotions pushed his self-control beyond its limits. Nan had always been quiet and well-behaved. Her difficulties in paying attention did not show up until third grade, when the academic content of her class notched up.

Schools are therefore usually heavily involved in the diagnosis of ADHD. The school system plays a major role in treatment until the child graduates from high school. As part of their training, school teachers and administrators need to know about ADHD and specific educational techniques that foster student success.[3] Finding the resources to bring the techniques into the classroom, and ensuring that everyone is knowledgeable about ADHD, are constant challenges for school systems.

In the case of a child who is not yet in school, a parent or caregiver may notice that the child seems more active, impulsive, or daydreamy than other children of the same age. Their first call will be to the family doctor. School systems offer programs to help children with behavioral and learning problems as young as age three.

## Many Tests

Since there is no single, clear-cut test for ADHD, information is gathered from many sources. For children in school, federal regulations require a comprehensive, unbiased evaluation to be completed. The evaluation must look at all aspects of the student's functioning: intellectual, behavioral, physical, and developmental. Federal law even specifies the members of the evaluation team: parents, at least one general education teacher and one special education teacher, someone qualified in the area of providing specially designed instruction, and someone who can translate the evaluation into instructional goals. Other specialists may be invited by the parents or the school. Doctors, psychologists, caregivers, and community members may be involved as needed.

## Physical

A general checkup comes first. Sometimes what looks like an attention problem turns out to be a physical defect that is fairly easily corrected.

There is no single clear-cut test for ADHD. For children, evaluation teams must examine all aspects of the student's functioning: intellectual, behavioral, physical, and developmental.

For example, some people appear not to be paying attention, when in fact they simply cannot hear well. A hearing test will determine if this is the case. A student in class may have problems seeing the blackboard and never look at it. This person needs glasses.

More subtle conditions such as auditory or visual processing problems may be causing what looks like inattention. In these situations, the ears or eyes do not need correction. However, the brain does not efficiently process the information it receives from the ears or eyes. A specialist must diagnose this type of processing disorder.[4]

Severe difficulty with mastering handwriting or being very clumsy might signal the need for an examination of the person's entire nervous system—reflexes, muscle strength and tone, balance, and the nerves leading into and out of the brain. It is important to screen for genetic disorders of development such as Fragile X, Turner, and Williams syndromes, all of which can all contribute to developing ADHD behaviors. Autism and mental retardation can also produce ADHD-like symptoms. Many doctors also check for allergies.[5]

## Educational

Nan's teacher completed several reports and checklists concerning her reading, writing, math skills, and behavior in class. Mrs. Hunter compared her behavior and performance to other students she has taught. The school counselor observed Nan in class several times.

Nan took a standardized IQ test as well as several individualized achievement tests. These tests have been taken by thousands of students across the country. By giving an idea of how the student's performance compares to the national average, they help identify specific areas of academic need. Finally, Nan's parents reported on her homework habits.

## Psychological

The psychologist at Nan's school asked her to complete some questionnaires, and then sat down to talk with her. They discussed her feelings about school, her family, her interests and hobbies. Dr. Jones was trying to find out if any serious problems such as anxiety or depression might be influencing Nan's academic situation. As they talked, Dr. Jones filled out a form that allowed him to compare her answers to national averages for other students her age.

## Environment

The biggest influence in most people's life is the family. This is especially true for children. Because of this fact, the school psychologist interviewed Nan's parents for over an hour. He asked about her health, from before birth until the present time. Her parents recalled that Nan had a lot of trouble sleeping as a baby. They talked about her school experiences, starting with preschool. Dr. Jones asked how she got along with her brother, her sister, and her friends. Finally, he asked if anyone else in the family ever had any academic or social problems.

Nan's parents also filled in several questionnaires. They answered questions about the home atmosphere, their own relationship, and their stress and anxiety levels.

## Coexisting Syndromes

One reason for the many tests that Nan took is the possibility that another disorder might be present, either instead of, or alongside of, ADHD. An accurate diagnosis of a problem is essential for effective treatment. Imagine being treated for a muscle pull when your arm is broken![6]

Some psychological disorders seem to occur frequently with ADHD. The relationship between the other disorder and ADHD is often very unclear. No one knows if one causes the other, or if they just happen to occur simultaneously in some people. These include oppositional/defiant disorder, in which a person constantly defies authority figures, conduct disorder, in which a person repeatedly violates normally accepted rules, as well as depression, anxiety, and bipolar disorder, formerly known as manic-depression.[7]

## Speech and Language Disorders

As many as one-third of children with difficulty under-standing and using language develop inattentive and hyperactive behaviors. For example, Jasper often could not think of the right words to use when his teacher called on him in class, although he knew the answer. In his frustration, he often made a stupid remark instead. Everybody thought he was a smart aleck, including his teacher. He felt very guilty about his behavior.

Dr. Phyllis Anne Teeter, a professor at the University of Wisconsin whose research focuses on ADHD, feels that difficulties in being able to express oneself, such as Jasper's, may be the cause of some ADHD behaviors. She points out that a child's ability to speak and to understand words grows along with his or her self-control. Part of growing up is learning to substitute language for action in the right circumstances. For instance, when your sister eats the piece of chocolate cake that you had been saving, how you react depends on how mature you are. A five-year-old might hit her. A fifteen-year-old will hopefully talk it out.

A person with a significant language problem may get so frustrated trying to communicate that he or she reverts to immature behavior, such as hitting or saying something inappropriate. A careful evaluation, like Jasper's, will uncover the language problem and allow it to be treated. In the process, the inappropriate behavior will probably improve.[8]

## Now What?

When all this testing is complete, what happens? In the cases of Nan and Jasper, each professional wrote a report, giving the results of the tests or interviews. The school psychologist put together a summary report and sent a copy to their parents.

All the information from the different sources must be carefully weighed. If any health problems were identified, they need treatment first. Similarly, if a psychological disorder that happens to cause ADHD behavior was identified, such as depression, it should be treated first. Only when these steps have been taken is ADHD considered as a possible cause of the problem behavior.[9]

In Nan's case, she turned out to be physically healthy, and did not suffer from any other psychological disorders. She did not have any other learning disabilities. Jasper's assessment found no psychological difficulties but uncovered a significant language disorder.

Both evaluation teams moved on to consider the possible diagnosis of ADHD. They were aware that many of the tests the students took and the questionnaires others filled out are subjective in nature. That is, they depend heavily on the viewpoint of the person giving the test or completing the questionnaire.[10] For instance, special education teachers typically find fewer problem behaviors when evaluating a child than regular education teachers. Parents under a great deal of stress from work or other sources also tend to report more behavior problems with their children than parents who are not under stress. Even when parents are not especially stressed, they often view their child's behavior very differently from the way the child's teacher sees it.[11]

When all the information was evaluated objectively, Nan still appeared more inattentive than other children her age, but was not at all hyperactive. Jasper, on the other hand, was quite

Parents, even when they are not especially stressed, often view their child's behavior very differently from the way the child's teacher sees it.

impulsive and hyperactive, and also experienced significant difficulty with language. He needed assistance in improving his language skills as well as in overcoming inattention and overactivity.

## DSM-IV

Most diagnoses of ADHD are made using the criteria, or standards, found in the *Diagnostic and Statistical Manual of Mental Disorders*. This widely used handbook, whose fourth edition is usually referred to as the DSM-IV, was written by many psychiatrists and psychologists belonging to the

# Diagnostic Criteria for Attention-Deficit/Hyperactivity Disorder[12]

◆ Either (1) or (2):

(1) six (or more) of the following symptoms of **inattention** have persisted for at least 6 months to a degree that is maladaptive and inconsistent with developmental level:

## *Inattention*

❖ often fails to give close attention to details or makes careless mistakes in schoolwork, work, or other activities

❖ often has difficulty sustaining attention in tasks or play activities

❖ often does not seem to listen when spoken to directly

❖ often does not follow through on instructions and fails to finish schoolwork, chores, or duties in the workplace (not due to oppositional behavior or failure to understand instructions)

❖ often has difficulty organizing tasks and activities

❖ often avoids, dislikes, or is reluctant to engage in tasks that require sustained mental effort (such as schoolwork or homework)

❖ often loses things necessary for tasks or activities (e.g., toys, school assignments, pencils, books, or tools)

❖ is often easily distracted by extraneous stimuli

❖ is often forgetful in daily activities

(2) six (or more) of the following symptoms of hyperactivity-impulsivity have persisted for at least 6 months to a degree that is maladaptive and inconsistent with developmental level:

## *Hyperactivity*

❖ often fidgets with hands or feet or squirms in seat

❖ often leaves seat in classroom or in other situations in which remaining seated is expected

# Diagnostic Criteria for Attention-Deficit/Hyperactivity Disorder[12] (cont.)

  ❖ often runs about or climbs excessively in situations in which it is inappropriate (in adolescents or adults, may be limited to subjective feelings of restlessness)
  ❖ often has difficulty playing or engaging in leisure activities quietly
  ❖ is often "on the go" or often acts as if "driven by a motor"
  ❖ often talks excessively

**Impulsivity**

  ❖ often blurts out answers before questions have been completed
  ❖ often has difficulty awaiting turn
  ❖ often interrupts or intrudes on others (e.g., butts into conversations or games)

◆ Some hyperactive-impulsive or inattentive symptoms that caused impairment were present before age 7.

◆ Some impairment from the symptoms is present in two or more settings (e.g., at school [or work] and at home).

◆ There must be clear evidence of clinically significant impairment in social, academic, or occupational functioning.

◆ The symptoms do not occur exclusively during the course of a Pervasive Developmental Disorder, Schizophrenia, or other Psychotic Disorder and are not better accounted for by another mental disorder (e.g., Mood Disorder, Anxiety Disorder, Dissociative Disorder, or a Personality Disorder).

American Psychiatric Association. It provides standards for diagnosing many psychological and behavioral disorders in children and adults. The fourth edition appeared in 1994.

The existence of an official diagnostic tool for ADHD does not mean that everyone agrees with it or uses it. For example, a doctor may find that a boy does not exhibit enough symptoms to qualify for a diagnosis according to the DSM-IV guidelines, but the few symptoms he has are severe. Does the boy have ADHD or not?

In order to help doctors and other practitioners working with ADHD, the American Academy of Pediatrics (APA), whose members are doctors working with children and adolescents, recently issued some advice about diagnosing ADHD.[13] The APA recommends that doctors use the DSM-IV standards as much as possible. However, the Academy warns that the standards have limitations. They do not take into account typical behavior differences between boys and girls. They ignore normal variations in children's growth and maturity. No mention is made in the DSM-IV of cultural differences. Finally, since behavior can never be fitted neatly into a standardized framework, practitioners must be very careful in making a diagnosis. The focus must stay on the person, not the criteria.

## Diagnosing Adults

Adults often unofficially diagnose themselves. They may spend a lot of time worrying about what might be wrong with them before finally going to their doctor or a counselor. The parent of a child diagnosed with ADHD frequently asks, do I also have ADHD?

Because of the increased awareness of the disorder, the number of adults requesting evaluations for ADHD is skyrocketing. However, diagnosing adults can be tricky. Adults typically show fewer obvious symptoms than children. They are usually less hyperactive. However, they may have severe problems in work and personal relationships. Psychological problems such as depression and anxiety are not uncommon alongside ADHD symptoms. Because ADHD is defined by the DSM-IV as a disorder beginning in childhood, adults who have ADHD symptoms are considered to have been undiagnosed in childhood.

The diagnostic procedure for adults is similar to that for children. An adult will usually consult the family doctor or a counselor and take some psychological tests, including an IQ test. Dr. Paul Wender of the University of Utah School of Medicine has developed an ADHD evaluation specifically for adults.[14] In addition to this evaluation, Dr. Wender finds that a review of school records can provide useful information even though the adult may no longer be in school. Interviews with a spouse and other relatives are conducted, when possible. The person's parents may be able to help, if they are still living. However, many adults choose not to disclose their symptoms and concerns to relatives and friends. Many fear losing their job or being shunned.

# 5

# Treating ADHD

One writer has said that people with ADHD are more different from each other than they are alike.[1] Nan, for instance, needed to study in an absolutely quiet place. Jasper wrote his best essays when his favorite music was blasting. Nan and Jasper are very different people. They need different treatment plans.

How does each child with ADHD and his or her parents decide which treatment or treatments will work best? Each family will discuss the results of the various medical and psychological evaluations with their family doctor and the school psychologist, and any other specialists they have consulted. They will be given a range of options—so many that they may feel overwhelmed. No one can say which ones will work best for a particular patient. However, almost everyone working with ADHD does agree that effective treatment for this complex disorder must address all aspects of the affected person's life: psychological, social, and educational or work-related. This is called multimodal treatment.[2]

A certain amount of trial and error is unavoidable in order to find the best combination of treatments. The time and cost of therapy and possible side effects from any medication all need to be considered. Good communication among all members of the team is essential for success. Treatments will change over time as the person gets older and as the situation changes.

## Family Treatments

Treatment for children and teenagers usually involves the family as a whole. A therapist or counselor works with the family to help identify issues and to work out solutions. Open, honest communication often needs to be nurtured. Since children model their behavior on that of their parents, it is important that parents have the ability to show their children what good behavior is.[3]

Specific home-based strategies include frequent, immediate, positive responses to good behavior. This is the "catch 'em when they're good" philosophy. A peaceful home atmosphere, where things get done on a predictable, regular schedule, promotes calmness. Realistic expectations are important—nobody is perfect! Posting a written list of chores in the refrigerator lets everybody know what needs to be done and when. Easily distracted children often complete their chores more efficiently when each task is broken into small parts.

## Social Skills Training

Many people with ADHD experience difficulty in social situations. Jasper's readiness to fight and sharp tongue caused many kids to keep their distance from him. Nan had more friends, but her tendency to daydream when they were talking to her made people think she was a little weird. She often forgot what they said to her because she was not really listening in the first place.

Most people with ADHD want to have friends. They want to be considerate and nice to others. They just have trouble controlling their reactions around others, especially if people do something that they do not like.

Role-playing different social situations with a trained counselor or therapist can help. What are good and bad ways to respond if someone cuts in front of you in line? How should you act at an upcoming social event? By practicing with a trained professional, a person with ADHD can learn to think through possible situations and form appropriate reactions before an event.

Sometimes people with ADHD have so much trouble dealing with other people that they just give up and become hermits. Sticking with small groups of people, or just one other person at a time, may be a good way to start making progress in socializing. Again, realistic expectations are important: one should not expect to give a speech to the entire high school population, but try talking to one person at lunch instead.

Many schools offer social skills groups through their counselors' offices. Sports and clubs can also provide opportunities to interact with other people.

## Cognitive Therapy

Jasper has benefited from a psychological approach called cognitive therapy. The goal of cognitive therapy is to help people use language rather than impulsive behavior in everyday situations. Twice a week he met with a group of other kids his own age, led by a counselor. The counselor presented them with a challenging situation and asked them to talk about handling it. They brainstormed solutions, first in small groups and then with the group as a whole. Jasper learned to talk himself calmly through events that, before, would have caused him to explode.[4]

## Individual Counseling

Many people with ADHD behavior have a long history of criticism from their parents, teachers, and friends.[5] They have probably experienced problems in all areas of their lives, starting at an early age. Constant negative feedback can batter and ultimately destroy a person's self-esteem. Building and maintaining positive self-esteem is the goal of individual counseling.[6] In individual counseling, a person may talk about problems and situations, role-play with the counselor, or even complete "assignments" such as talking to two new people a week.

This type of therapy can be particularly helpful if the person is struggling with depression, anxiety, abuse, or other problems.

## Diet and Exercise

Dr. Ben Feingold, a pediatrician and chief of the Department of Allergy at Kaiser Medical Care Program in northern California in the 1950s and 1960s, proposed that artificial food colorings and flavors, as well as food preservatives and artificial sweeteners, cause or aggravate ADHD symptoms in many children. He noticed that these food additives were not widely used until after the Second World War. This is when reported cases of ADHD began to rise. He recommended a diet free of these substances, as well as some naturally occurring chemicals that he felt could intensify ADHD behaviors.[7] No rigorous studies of this theory have been conducted, since it is difficult to know exactly what is in the food we eat. Still, there is evidence that some people find that their hyperactivity and inattention decrease when they eliminate these things from their diets.[8]

Plain, old-fashioned sugar has also been named a culprit in many illnesses, from diabetes to obesity and depression to fatigue.[9] Again, there is no hard and fast evidence that too much sugar causes hyperactivity, but many mothers swear it does! It is important to use good judgment when changing dietary habits, and to follow common-sense guidelines.

Exercise is an obvious, but often overlooked outlet for a hyperactive person. Research suggests that exercise increases the production of endorphins, which are chemicals in the brain that promote a sense of calmness and well-being. Track, soccer, gymnastics, and other sports help channel energy that might otherwise burst out inappropriately. The routine and discipline required of many sports, such as martial arts or ballet, can also assist in focusing.[10]

Some doctors recommend vitamin supplements, such as magnesium, vitamin B6, niacin, and zinc.[11] No scientific studies confirm their effectiveness, but some people find them helpful. Another experimental treatment for ADHD symptoms is biofeedback. In a biofeedback session, a person watches a monitor of his or her bodily functions such as heart rate, muscle tension, and brainwave activity, and learns to control them voluntarily. It is thought that learning to control these functions helps a person control his or her reactions and behavior.

## Medication

If behavioral and other interventions do not produce improvement in behavior, a trial run of medication may be considered. Medications for ADHD are not "brain candy," or "chill pills," as some people call them. They are serious drugs, which affect the workings of the brain and the entire body. Close supervision by a medical doctor is essential for medication to work safely and properly.

The routine and discipline required of many sports can help children with ADHD to focus.

# Stimulants

Stimulants are the most commonly administered medication for ADHD symptoms. Probably the most widely prescribed is methylphenidate, or Ritalin.

Stimulants are psychotropic, or mood-altering drugs. They work by regulating the levels of certain chemicals in the brain. These chemicals, known as neurotransmitters, help information travel in the brain. Brain cells do not actually touch each other. A cell with information to transmit sends chemicals into the gap between itself and another cell that are sensed by the next cell. For the chemical connection to click, the right level of the right neurotransmitter must be present in the gap, which is called the synapse. Some medications increase the amount of chemical in the synapse. Others prevent the chemicals from being absorbed too quickly, before the information is passed.

The right level of these chemicals quiets the "background noise" in the brain so a person can pay attention to something. If there is too much background noise, the person gets confused and just zones out. In ADHD terms, the person becomes inattentive. Confusion can then lead to frustration and impulsive actions.

Ritalin and other stimulants are taken orally, in pill form. The dosage is adjusted according to a person's response. Doctors try to keep the dose as low as possible. These medications are absorbed into the bloodstream and pass quickly into the brain. The effects of stimulants generally last three to four hours, although longer-acting versions are available. Side effects are rare, but include insomnia, loss of appetite, irritability, anxiety, stomachaches, and headaches. These drugs can also increase the heart rate, blood pressure, and electrical activity in the brain. Occasionally, a person develops tics, or uncontrollable twitchings, when taking stimulant medication.[12]

## Antidepressants

The group of medications known as tricyclic antidepressants are sometimes used to treat ADHD when stimulants do not work. They can be helpful for people who also experience depression. They may cause dry mouth or sleepiness in some people.

Another type of antidepressants known as selective serotonin reuptake inhibitors, or SSRIs, is being used more frequently to treat ADHD behaviors, often in combination with a stimulant. The best known of this class of medication is Prozac. SSRIs work by regulating the level of a brain chemical called serotonin in the brain. Lower than normal levels of serotonin occur in people who suffer from depression, anxiety, and obsessive-compulsive behaviors. Side effects of SSRI antidepressants include dry mouth, blurred vision, and headaches.

Although antidepressant medications are not specifically approved to treat ADHD symptoms, they do help some people who have ADHD, especially if they suffer from some of the other disorders mentioned.[13]

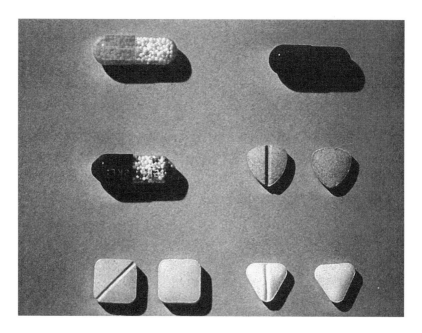

Medication helps many of those with ADHD, making a big difference in their lives. It calms them down, makes them less impulsive, and helps them pay attention in class and at work.

## The Multimodal Treatment Study

The National Institute of Mental Health (NIMH) is part of the National Institutes of Health (NIH) in Washington, D.C. Both are government agencies that sponsor research and education on public health issues. NIMH and NIH have been studying the problems of defining and treating ADHD. Recently, NIMH sponsored a study of 579 children aged seven to nine with ADHD. Children from seven different areas in the United States and Canada were randomly assigned to one of four treatments: 1) medication alone; 2) psychosocial/behavioral treatment alone; 3) a combination of 1 and 2; 4) routine community care. The study evaluated children over a period of fourteen months.

Results of the study suggest that a combination of psychological and behavioral counseling with medication is the most effective overall treatment. Medication alone was more helpful than behavioral treatments alone. Combination treatment helped more than the others in the areas of anxiety, academic performance, uncooperative behavior, parent-child relations, and social skills. The combination of treatments also allowed for lower levels of medication.[14]

## To Medicate or Not To Medicate?

The role of medication in treating ADHD symptoms is highly controversial. No medication can actually cure ADHD. Although the medications are not supposed to be addictive, some people have found them easy to abuse.

In a 1997 survey of high school students in a Midwestern town, 7 percent admitted using Ritalin "for fun" at least once in the previous year. The danger in this "recreational" use lies in the fact that most abusers take a much higher dose than is recommended. High doses of any stimulant can cause convulsions, nervousness, insomnia, and mental disturbance.[15]

Most people taking medication for ADHD do not abuse it. However, the potential for abuse is always there.[16]

Another cause for controversy over medications for ADHD is the lack of research on the effects of the medications, especially when they are taken for a long time. Many of

# Questions To Ask About Taking Medication[17]

◆ What target symptoms is the medication supposed to help?

◆ When do I go back to the doctor?

◆ What are the effects and side effects of this drug? When are they serious enough for me to call the doctor?

◆ What if I don't like the effects? What other options do I have?

◆ How long do I have to take this medication before I see results?

◆ What other drugs or foods should I avoid when taking this medication?

the drugs are new, and there has not yet been time to carry out long-term studies. None of these medications is approved for very young children, yet the number of two- to four-year-olds receiving stimulants and antidepressants rose 50 percent between 1991 and 1995.[18] Combining medications is a relatively new procedure, and there is a lack of long-term studies to provide guidance on proper usage.

NIMH has established seven research units on pediatric psychopharmacology in university clinics across the United States, which have as their goal the study of the effects and

# Commonly Prescribed Medications For ADHD[19]

## Stimulants
Ritalin® (methylphenidate)
Dexedrine® (dextroamphetamine)
Adderall® (amphetamine)
Desoxyn® (methamphetamine)
Cylert® (magnesium pemoline)

### Indications and Side Effects
Usually tried first
Effects are short-term
Side effects include insomnia,
   poor appetite, headache,
   stomach ache

## Tricyclic Antidepressants
Tofranil® (imipramine hydrochloride)
Norpramin® (desipramine hydrochloride)
Pamelor® (nortriptyline hydrochloride)
Elavil® (amitriptyline hydrochloride)
Anafranil® (clomipramine)

### Indications and Side Effects
Helpful with depression, anxiety
May worsen heart irregularities

## Selective Serotonin Reuptake Inhibitors (SSRIs)
Prozac® (fluoexetine)
Zoloft® (sertraline)
Paxil® (paroexetine)
Luvox® (fluvoxamine)

### Indications and Side Effects
Helpful with coexisting depression
   or anxiety
Side effects include dry mouth,
   vision problems, headache
   nausea, sleep disturbance

## Antihypertensives (High Blood Pressure Medications)
Catapres® (clonidine)
Tenex® (guanfacine)

### Indications and Side Effects
Helpful with tic disorders

## Other
Wellbutrin® (buproprion)

safety of medications such as Ritalin and Prozac on children. One focus of the study will be the possible long-term effects.[20]

Some people do not like to take drugs that affect their feelings and behavior. They prefer to feel that they, and not a pill, are in control. Many school-aged children do not like their peers to know that they are taking a pill in order to behave properly.[21]

# 6

# Strategies for Success in School

**H**elping children in school with ADHD requires cooperation among teachers, parents, and students with and without ADHD. In many instances, the law specifies how help is to be provided in school.

## ADHD and Education Laws

Federal, state, and local laws governing the education of people with disabilities have been used to help students with ADHD receive assistance in school. A diagnosis of ADHD does not automatically make a student eligible for special education services. The child must be found to have one or more physical or mental impairments specified by law which cause the child to need special education services.[1]

69

Laws to ensure a fair education for people with disabilities date back to the 1820s.[2] The United States Congress has passed many pieces of legislation trying to help the individual states develop special education services and train teachers. These laws provide the framework for evaluating and assisting school-aged children with ADHD.

Since 1991, the federal government has considered children with ADHD to be eligible for special education services under two different laws. The first is the Individuals with Disabilities Education Act, known as IDEA. This law first appeared as the Education for All Handicapped Children Act in 1975, and has been revised several times since then. IDEA does not classify ADHD as a separate disability. It has placed ADHD under the "other health impaired" disability category since 1991.[3]

IDEA is a package of laws designed to assure that all students with disabilities have the right to a free, appropriate public education. It sets forth specific methods for students and their parents to gain this education, and helps state and local education agencies provide it. It also makes federal funding available for the states to use in special education.

If a student does not qualify under the IDEA definition of a disability, she or he may qualify under the provisions of a different law. Section 504 of the Rehabilitation Act of 1973 prohibits discrimination on the basis of handicap for institutions that receive federal funds, such as schools. Under this law, "handicap" is defined as "a physical or mental impairment which substantially limits a major life activity (e.g., learning)." Thus, students with milder forms of ADHD may receive some special education services under this law. However, no federal funds are available for services provided through Section 504.[4]

## The Law In Action

If the student falls under the Section 504 criteria for mental or physical handicap, a "504 Student Accommodation Plan" is worked out. Parents and teachers, counselors and other school personnel meet to develop a coordinated series of goals and strategies to help the student toward academic success. This plan is somewhat informal. Section 504 plans are normally reviewed once a year.

If the student's learning and/or behavioral challenges are more severe, the school follows the IDEA regulations.

## Individual Education Plans

If the evaluation reveals that the student meets the criteria for a disability according to the IDEA definition, the next step is to write an Individual Education Program (IEP). An IEP must be written at least once a year, but always before the beginning of a new school year. It is revised as often as necessary. This plan, more formal in nature than a 504 Plan, constitutes a contract between the school and the student and parents.

An IEP may take up many pages. Many people participate in the development of these programs: regular and special education teachers, a school administrator with special qualifications in writing such plans, parents, and other specialists as appropriate. At Nan's IEP meeting, Mrs. Hunter, Dr. Jones, Mrs. Smith, a math specialist, the principal of her school, and her parents were all present. Jasper attended his own IEP meeting, although he did not like listening to people talk about him.

An IEP has several components. It begins with a statement of how the student is doing in school at the present time. Then it specifies measurable annual goals related to meeting the student's needs, what methods and services will be used to reach the goals, and how progress toward the goals will be measured.[5]

After the initial evaluation, a reevaluation is completed every three years, or whenever the student's situation changes, or if a parent or teacher requests a reevaluation.[6]

The school system may become involved in helping children before they enter school, if they meet the IDEA criteria for a disability. For these children, the plan is called an Individualized Family Service Plan (IFSP). School personnel may or may not be involved in this plan. Intervention focuses on the child in the family situation, although a child may receive speech therapy or other services in a school setting.

# Strategies for Success

Once the goals have been defined, the focus shifts to defining ways to meet them. Strategies and accommodations must be tailored to the individual student. They will vary by age and educational goals.[7]

# General

All teachers, administrators, students, and parents need to know about ADHD.

- All teachers, administrators, students, and parents need to avoid labeling.

- An environment of kindness and cooperation at school lets everyone feel accepted.

- Immediate, positive reinforcement, rather than negative criticism, creates and sustains motivation for success.

- A calm, structured environment promotes attention.

- Close communication between school and home reinforces school strategies at home.

- Hands-on assignments and tasks maintain student interest.

- Changes in routine, such as computer-assisted instruction, help keep a student's attention.

- One-on-one instruction may be necessary to teach difficult subjects.

- Clear, easily understood expectations let everyone know where they stand.

- Short, varied tasks can inspire interest. As the student matures, he or she can learn to break a large task like a book report into several workable steps.

- Adjust assignments, time for tests, and grading procedures if necessary.

- Maintain a sense of humor!

## Elementary School

After the IEP meeting, Nan's teacher changed the format of Nan's math homework. She gave her the same overall number

Understanding teachers are important to children with ADHD and their parents.

of problems, but put fewer problems on each page. Nan was not distracted by all the numbers on the pages and was able to complete her homework every night.

Mrs. Hunter also moved Nan away from the window. She paired all the students in the class with "study buddies" for some assignments. For Nan's buddy, she picked a well-organized student.

Finally, Mrs. Hunter arranged a secret signal with Nan. If Mrs. Hunter saw that Nan was not paying attention, she would tap Nan lightly on the shoulder. This little gesture told Nan to bring her focus back to the material in the class. No one else noticed what Mrs. Hunter was doing, because she moved around the class while teaching. Nan's concentration in class improved without her being embarrassed by public reminders.

## Middle and High School

Jasper's teachers decided to allow him to get up and walk around occasionally in class, as long as he was quiet about it and stayed in the back of the room. They also agreed to check his assignment notebook before he left class, to be sure he had written everything down.

To help Jasper become more comfortable answering when he was called on in class, several teachers experimented with different teaching methods, such as question-and-answer, computer-assisted instruction, and student-led presentations. One teacher conducted a session of role-playing, in which the students explored the effects of the different methods and their

Teachers can experiment with different teaching methods such as question-and-answer, computer-assisted instruction, and student-led presentations.

responses with all the students in class. The students learned that there are many different learning styles, and they learned to be patient with people who learn and respond differently. As a result, all the students felt more comfortable participating in class.

A student in Jasper's homeroom class came over and helped him organize his desk at home, and talked to him once a week about his homework and study habits. Jasper was nervous about getting help from this quiet, "brainy" boy, but the two became friends when it turned out that the other boy had always admired Jasper's "cool" persona and athletic ability. Jasper helped him make the soccer team.

## What If We Don't Agree?

If parents and the school disagree about the services to be provided by the school, part of the IDEA regulations provides a structure to work out the conflict. Parents may ask for an independent evaluation if they feel their child's disability has not been properly understood by the school. Mediation and due process hearings are available to ensure the right educational experience for the child.

It is not uncommon for differences of opinion to arise in the process of finding the best educational placement for a child. Many parents find the process of working out educational services and making sure they are delivered exhausting and frustrating. Open communication and persistence are important in making the process work. Bringing a friend or advocate along to school meetings can make the meetings less stressful. Advocates who specialize in helping families work through the special education process are available.[8]

## What About College?

More and more students with various kinds of learning disabilities and/or ADHD are attending college. In 1998, 154,520 freshmen, 9.4 percent of all full-time, first-year college students, disclosed some kind of disability. About half identified the disability as a learning disability, a category that includes ADHD. In contrast, less than 3 percent disclosed any disability in 1978.[9]

The laws governing accommodations for disabilities are somewhat different at the college level. The IDEA laws cover students through high school, but not in college. Colleges are not legally required to provide accommodation or support for a disability unless a student asks. This represents a change from elementary and high school, where the schools must actively seek children with learning difficulties and make accommodations.

Colleges do not have to reduce admission standards or graduation requirements for disabled students, but they must be sure they do not discriminate on the basis of the disability. This means they must make necessary changes in classes and exams, but do not have to provide remedial services, such as tutoring.[10]

At the college level, students must take an active role in identifying their needs and requesting services. Some examples of helpful interventions for college students with ADHD include:[11]

- taking fewer courses per semester
- sitting near the instructor
- tape-recording lectures
- using a note-taker in class
- extended time on exams

- taking exams orally
- taking exams in a distraction-free environment

Increasing public awareness of ADHD and learning disabilities has led to more options for students. More and more colleges have learning-support staff available to students. Landmark College in Putney, Vermont, is a two-year college that accepts only students with learning disabilities and/or ADHD. Its goal is to prepare students to transfer to a four-year college and succeed. Landmark enrolled 340 students in 1999, and its enrollment is growing.

# 7

# ADHD and Society

**M**ike's wife was very upset. It was her turn to make dinner, so she had asked him what he wanted before they left for work in the morning. "Fried chicken," he said. Cathy had spent an hour over a hot, greasy frying pan when Mike walked in the door with a pizza box in his hand.

"Pizza looked good," he explained as he sat down to eat, straight from the box. "What are you making?"

This was not the first time Mike has abruptly changed his mind about dinner. He did it with other things, too. Cathy could never choose birthday or holiday gifts for Mike. He changed his mind a million times. She decided just to buy gift certificates.

Mike used to forget to pay his bills. Cathy took over the family finances, but ran into trouble when Mike forgot to give her his paycheck, or forgot to tell her he had just bought a new set of premium tires for his work truck and there was no paycheck this week. Cathy knew Mike was lucky to be receiving a paycheck at all. He was just as forgetful and impulsive on the job as he was at home. He had a very understanding boss.

Despite all the aggravation, Cathy did not want Mike to change. She loved his constant, thoughtful surprises. Last year he flew her brother out as a surprise for her birthday. Mike was kind, loving, and considerate, in his own quirky way. Cathy just tried to be patient as she washed the frying pan out.

## ADHD and Adults

For a long time, people thought that kids outgrew ADHD, and that the problems went away when a person became an adult. Cathy knew that Mike had been diagnosed with ADHD as a child. She did not know much about ADHD, but she had a vague feeling that it was a problem for children, not adults.

We now know that this is not always true. The most noticeable symptom, hyperactivity, does generally decrease as a person grows up. But two-thirds of adults who displayed ADHD behaviors as children still have some ADHD symptoms as adults.[1] There are no statistics on cases of adult ADHD, but their number is rising dramatically.[2]

Many adults with ADHD function well. Adulthood brings with it more opportunities for individual strengths and interests than school years.[3] However, adults with ADHD often work harder than other adults at their jobs, at home, and in the community. Organizational problems, including putting

81

<br>

# Lifelong ADHD

Chris Knight played cute little Peter on the Brady Bunch. The TV audience loved his mischievous, sweet character. What they did not know was how hard it was for him to calm down enough to act, and to remember his lines. Years after the show ended, he was diagnosed as having lifelong ADHD. Now he says, "everything made sense." He has a new career and feels his best years are still to come.[4]

things off, often plague ADHD sufferers. Adults may speak without thinking, causing pain and embarrassment. Some are impatient and easily frustrated when things do not go their way. They may give up quickly at work or in relationships.

We all know people who get easily bored with the daily routine, and constantly seek ways to spice it up. They may move frequently or change jobs as often as others change the oil in their cars. This habit can upset a person's family, especially if the decision to change is made on a whim. Financial security can be affected by frequent job changes.

A more dangerous form of this behavior is thrill-seeking. Driving too fast or not filing income taxes may make a person feel he is living "on the edge," when he is really taking unnecessary chances. Again, these behaviors affect more than just the person taking chances.

Some adults are so overwhelmed with their lack of organization and the results that flow from it that they try to deaden their pain and despair with alcohol or drugs. This type of "self-medicating" is extremely destructive.

## ADHD on the Job

ADHD behaviors can interfere with a person's ability to find and keep a job. A "good fit" between a person's personality and skills and the work he or she chooses to do is always the key to success on the job, but doubly so when ADHD is involved. Fortunately, studies show that adults who were

Driving too fast or not filing income taxes may make a person feel he is living on the edge.

83

Using alcohol or illicit drugs to deal with overwhelming stress is extremely destructive.

diagnosed with ADHD as children are just as likely to be employed as adults without any history of ADHD.[5]

A formal skill and aptitude inventory can help identify good career choices. Many adults with ADHD find that a job with a variety of tasks, not one basic routine, and many new challenges fits their work style best. Sometimes a work routine that involves physical activity is also good. Jobs that require long periods of sitting or stillness or a high degree of customer contact may not work out well. ADHD individuals often own their own businesses.

Mike was lucky to find a boss who could work around his forgetfulness and sometimes unpredictable behavior. Others may have more difficulty in the job arena. A law was passed in 1990 to help people who are able to work but who have mental or learning-related disabilities that interfere with their job duties. This law is called the Americans with Disabilities Act (ADA).

The ADA was originally written to protect workers with physical disabilities. However, it has been extended to include psychiatric and emotional conditions. ADHD is not specifically included as a disability by the ADA, but if the ADHD symptoms significantly interfere with one's ability to perform major life activities such as concentrating, working with others, and learning, then the provisions of the ADA apply.

The ADA does not allow employers to ask job applicants if they have a mental disability. Also, it requires employers to change work schedules or the work environment to help a worker concentrate or learn job duties. It is important to realize that some employers may resent having to make these changes, due to their cost and the inconvenience they create.[6]

A few jobs, such as a commercial pilot, are not open to applicants taking any kind of medication. The military is not required to consider applicants who take medications for ADHD. But these types of jobs are in the minority.

## ADHD and the Family

ADHD behaviors can place a strain not just on the individual, but on parents, brothers and sisters, children, and friends. ADHD behaviors can create stress for every member of a family. Without a complete understanding of the issues, parents may blame themselves and each other for their child's actions and condition. They may spend so much time monitoring and responding to their active child that they have no time for each other, or themselves.

Brothers and sisters may feel ignored when the more demanding child gets all the attention. They feel jealous because the "difficult" kid is getting all the attention, or angry because they have to take care of the "ADHD kid." Part of a counselor's role is to provide information about ADHD to every member of the family.

Defending a child's behavior or school performance to grandparents, angry neighbors, or even strangers in the supermarket is exhausting. Working with the school can also be draining. Evaluations and treatments may be costly and time-consuming.

When another child, or one or both parents, shows ADHD symptoms, the picture gets even more complicated. In such cases, family systems treatment, which helps the family work together as a whole, is often recommended.[7]

## Help for Adults

Adults require multimodal treatment, including behavioral therapy, social skills training, and possibly medication. Medications, including stimulants, have been found to help but may not work as effectively on adults as on children.[8]

Many adults have additional difficulties, such as depression or learning disabilities. People who are not diagnosed

People with ADHD may engage in activities that are risky.

with ADHD until adulthood may require therapy to work through the conflicts and lack of success they experienced while growing up. Treating the additional disorder may help the ADHD symptoms.[9]

Learning to communicate with others is often difficult for people with ADHD. Unwritten social rules may pass them by. Social skills training can help. Simple improvements in organizational skills, like following a daily routine and using a date book or calendar, can make a big difference. A spouse or a close friend can help keep the person on track.[10] Many people are turning to job coaches, who help people with ADHD analyze their tasks at home and on the job and develop systems and strategies to succeed.[11]

It is hard to measure the cost of ADHD to society. We do know that ADHD medication for children and adults costs $670 million a year in the United States.[12] This figure accounts for only a small part of the total cost of the disorder. The cost of evaluations, accommodations, doctor visits, and therapy is impossible to determine at this point. Underemployment, days lost at work, substance abuse, family problems, and divorce all cost millions of dollars.

## Don't Ask, Don't Tell

Mike has never told anyone that he had ADHD as a child. He is afraid he will be passed over for promotion at work, or even fired. He is also afraid that his friends will think he is weird.

Nan also found the ADHD label embarrassing. She felt she now belonged to a community of "undesirables." Still, she was glad she was doing better in school.

Jasper, on the other hand, celebrated when he received the ADHD diagnosis. Finally, other people would understand that his awkward behavior and social problems were not his fault.

The decision to disclose ADHD is personal. Labeling may create a self-fulfilling prophecy of failure if ADHD is thought of as a purely biological condition that can never improve. Since it is also a psychiatric disorder, as defined by the DSM-IV, it may bring the stigma of mental illness to the person who has it. However, it may bring relief to those who finally have an explanation for the behaviors they could never control. When others understand that a person's behavior is related to ADHD, relationships can dramatically improve.

# 8

# The Future and ADHD

**W**hy is the number of ADHD cases skyrocketing? Why is it so high in the Western world, particularly the United States?

These questions have no solutions at the present time. The answers probably lie in two main areas: the workings of the brain, and the effect of changes in Western society on personality.

## Research

Science today is making tremendous strides in understanding brain chemistry and structure. Many of the findings are helping us understand ADHD better.

## Genetic Research

The discovery that a tendency toward ADHD behavior runs in families has spurred researchers to look for the specific genes that pass this tendency from one generation to the next. It is likely that the genetic cause of ADHD behaviors will be found not in a single gene, but in a combination of genes.

Even if a genetic tendency toward ADHD behavior is identified, no one can predict the form it will take in an individual. However, if genetic testing reveals a high risk for ADHD in a family, the family can take steps early in a child's life to prevent many of the negative effects of ADHD on the child and the family.[1]

## Brain Structure

Several MRI studies have been conducted to find out whether the actual structure of the brain plays a part in ADHD. Several slight differences in structure in various parts of the brain have been noted. One study measured the size of the *corpus callosum,* a "bridge" of nerve cells that allows the right and left sides of the brain to communicate with each other. Learning, memory, and attention are all shared between the two hemispheres through the *corpus callosum.* In people with more severe ADHD symptoms, this "bridge" was found to be slightly smaller than in people without severe ADHD symptoms.[2]

Studies made of the brain while it is in the process of paying attention are just in the early stages. The latest technique, functional Magnetic Resonance Imaging (fMRI), allows researchers to look at the brain in action without the use of radioactive material required by Positron Emission Topography (PET) scans. This technique holds great promise for the future.[3]

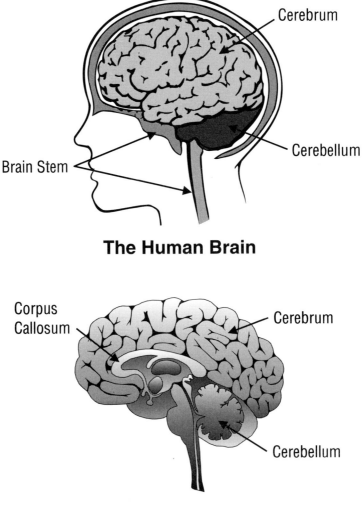

**The Human Brain**

**Cross-section of the Human Brain**

The corpus callosum, a "bridge" of nerve cells, allows the right and left sides of the brain to communicate with each other. In people with more severe ADHD symptoms, this "bridge" was found to be slightly smaller than in people without severe ADHD symptoms.

# The Environment

Much more research is needed on the effects of a person's environment on ADHD, and on which environmental treatments work best. Environments are usually defined as school, home, community, and work. Each of these situations can be very complex. Treatments in these situations will also be complex.

One reason for the lack of research in this area is that it is extremely hard to define and measure environmental factors. When Jasper was being evaluated, for instance, his teachers had to decide whether he fidgeted "never," "occasionally," "sometimes," "often," or "always." They found these categories very difficult to pinpoint.

Also, a person's environment may change in many ways at one time. For example, a student may have an argument with her best friend, forget her homework, and come home to find that her grandmother is in the hospital. Keeping track of all of these changes, not to mention charting their effects, may be impossible.

# Biology and Environment

Recently, researchers in England conducted a study of mice which had been bred to have Huntington's disease. In humans, this brain disorder destroys the ability to walk, talk, and think. Half of the mice with the Huntington's gene were kept in standard, comfortable cages with plenty of food and bedding. The other half lived in cages with lots of interesting toys and objects—tunnels, boxes, and tubes—made of cardboard, paper, and plastic. The items were changed every few days to insure variety. The mice living in the environment with the constantly changing toys developed fewer symptoms of the disease, and developed them more slowly, than the mice in the standard cages.[4]

This research suggests that the environment has a marked influence on brain chemistry. Such findings may explain why the environment has such an effect on the intensity and frequency of a person's ADHD symptoms.

## What Is It?

The National Institutes of Health recently issued a consensus statement naming ADHD as a "costly major public health problem" whose diagnosis and treatment are still controversial. Despite years of research, we still do not know what causes ADHD.[6] It is therefore no surprise that some professionals working with ADHD claim that it is not a medical or psychiatric disorder.[7] It is interesting that the definition of ADHD in the most official diagnostic tool, the DSM, has been revised three times since it first appeared in 1965. Thomas Armstrong, the author of seven books on parenting and education, is not the first to point out that the definitions of all illnesses, including psychiatric illnesses, change as society changes.[8]

Dr. Lawrence Diller, a California pediatrician who has worked with many children with ADHD, feels the explanation for the rise in ADHD diagnoses may lie in our society's

# The Environment and ADHD

There is also evidence that the environment can change the structure of the brain.

If you've ever been to London, chances are you took a cab to get around the city. London cab drivers are justly famous for their knowledge of the tiniest, twistiest streets in the city. Researchers at University College, London, compared the cabbies' brains to those of ordinary Londoners. They discovered that one part of the cabbies' brains is larger than the same part in other people. This area is the rear hippocampus, a part of the brain associated with navigation. All the driving the cabbies do has actually enlarged their brains![5]

increasing expectations for our children. Naturally, parents want their children to be successful and happy. Nowadays, this means going to a "good" college in order to get a "good" job. The quest for success starts early: competition to get into a "good" preschool can be fierce. So the cute little fireball running around the playground dumping toys is no longer considered to be just acting like a kid. He is diagnosed with a medical disorder and receives medication and therapy before his typical three-year-old's behavior can ruin his future.

Other changes in our society also come into play. Today, many people move far away from their families and friends in order to move up the employment and social ladder. Their children have few family and community supports. Schools are expected to do much of the job of parenting, in spite of increasing financial pressures and restrictions. The stress level at home is high. There is no time for a child to behave "differently." Hyperactivity is not addressed, but is medicated away.[9]

The apparent advantages to a medical diagnosis of ADHD can be hard to resist. Stimulants increase everyone's concentration. The extra help at school and untimed testing on exams, including the SAT, make some parents actually eager for such a diagnosis for their child.[10]

Dr. Diller sees the surge in ADHD diagnoses and medication as a warning that we as a society are not meeting the needs of our children. Adults are struggling as well. He wonders if we are labeling normal behaviors like inattention and activity "ADHD," and then trying to control them through medication in order to remain "normal" as life becomes increasingly complex.[11]

## The Role of Medication

Most professionals feel that medication is only one part of treatment for ADHD and should not normally be used alone. Dr. Russell Barkley, professor of Psychiatry and Neurology at the University of Massachusetts Medical Center, feels that "for most cases . . . the greatest benefit of stimulant therapy seems to be its ability to increase the effectiveness of psychological and educational treatments."[12] However, a review of both environmental and medical treatments available for ADHD from 1989 to 1996

## Too Much Attention?

Matthew Melmed, the director of Zero To Three, National Center for Infants, Toddlers, and Families, feels that parents who spent short but intense periods of time with their children may be setting the children up for problems in paying attention later in life. Research conducted at the center shows that babies and young children learn more from the hours in the ordinary routine of life than from fifteen minutes of overwhelming stimulation from a guilty parent. Too much stimulation may push children further than they are capable of going and harm their long-term development.[13]

found a significant decrease in the amount of non-medical counseling and follow-up care for children with ADHD. One monitoring organization reported that the total number of prescriptions dispensed in the United States for ADHD drugs increased a staggering 81.2 percent between June 1994 and June 1998.[14] The reviewers felt that factors such as waiting lists to see doctors, a lack of specialists, and problems with insurance coverage all interfered with children's ability to receive good care for ADHD symptoms.[15]

## Not Such a Bad Thing

Many professionals see ADHD as simply one point along the continuum of human behavior.[16] Thom Hartmann, the author of four books on ADHD, proposes the intriguing theory that ADHD behaviors developed early in the evolution of the human race to ensure survival. Distractibility was originally the ability to constantly scan one's surroundings for danger or opportunity. Quick, impulsive actions ensured that the person responded immediately in the dangerous situation, or took advantage of an opportunity, such as dinner standing on four legs a few feet away. Risk-taking evolved to help hunters catch more game.[17]

Jasper, like many others with an ADHD diagnosis, feels more positive about himself now. Some people call him hyper. He thinks of himself as energetic. He has more creative ideas than anyone he knows. He has started writing music instead of just listening to it. He still wants to fly

Many famous people, including Albert Einstein, are believed to have had ADHD.

airplanes. He knows he can accomplish whatever he sets his mind to.

An awareness of ADHD requires all of us to try new ways of looking at tasks, behaviors, and each other. It can be a springboard to accepting our diversity as human beings. People such as Thomas Alva Edison, Albert Einstein, and Wolfgang Amadeus Mozart, among many others, may have had symptoms of ADHD.[18] It did not stop them from achieving success.

# Q & A

**Q.** What causes ADHD?

**A.** No one knows. It appears to be caused by a combination of biological factors and environmental influences.

**Q.** What is the difference between ADHD and ADD?

**A.** Some people use the term ADD to describe only the impulsive, inattentive, and distracted features of this disorder, and ADHD when including its hyperactive component. Others use the term AD/HD, indicating that hyperactivity is not always present.

**Q.** Who gets ADHD?

**A.** Children, adults, boys, and girls all have ADHD. Boys are diagnosed more frequently than girls. Children are diagnosed more frequently than adults, because they tend to be more hyperactive and thus get noticed more. ADHD does not seem to occur more frequently in specific ethnic or economic groups.

**Q.** Do drugs cure ADHD?

**A.** No drug has yet been discovered that can cure ADHD. Some medications improve the symptoms in certain people. When the drugs are stopped, however, the improvement usually stops, also.

**Q.** Can ADHD be prevented?

**A.** Because the cause of ADHD is unknown, we do not yet know how to prevent it. However, early identification and treatment in children may prevent ADHD symptoms from becoming severe as the children get older.

**Q.** Does ADHD go away when a person grows up?

**A.** About two-thirds of all children with ADHD still experience some symptoms as adults. The hyperactive component, if present, tends to diminish or go away as a person grows up. People identified with ADHD as adults often recall having had symptoms as children.

**Q.** Does having ADHD mean you're a "bad" kid?

**A.** No. It means you need to work harder at paying attention and regulating your behavior than most of your peers. It means you might benefit from counseling and medication.

**Q.** Can I catch ADHD by being around someone who has it?

**A.** Absolutely not. ADHD is the name for a group of behaviors. It is not a disease, infection, or virus.

**Q.** If I have ADHD, will my children have it too?

**A.** A tendency toward ADHD behaviors does appear to be passed from generation to generation. There is no way to predict whether your children will have ADHD if you do. You may want to have them evaluated early if you see any ADHD behaviors.

**Q.** I do not like taking medication to behave. Can I stop?

**A.** All medication must be taken under a doctor's supervision. Similarly, stopping all medication must be done with a doctor's permission. Talk to your parents and doctor about your feelings. Perhaps you are ready to stop taking medication, or maybe you can take less.

**Q.** I forget things a lot and can't sit still. Do I have ADHD?

**A.** ADHD is diagnosed only after a thorough evaluation that looks at your behavior in many different situations. If you feel you might have ADHD, talk to your parents. They can request an evaluation from your doctor or through your school.

**Q.** Does ADHD really exist, or are people merely making excuses for their behavior?

**A.** You are not alone in your uncertainty. Because ADHD is so difficult to pin down, some people doubt it exists. However, it is clear that many people do experience inattentive, impulsive, and hyperactive behaviors, sometimes to a severe degree. Most of these people benefit from treatment for ADHD.

**Q.** My best friend just found out she has ADHD. What should I do?

**A.** Take your cue from your friend. Let her tell you about it, and don't be afraid to ask her questions. Let her know you still like her just the way she is. And don't tell anyone else unless she says it's okay.

# ADHD Timeline

**400 B.C.**—Greek doctors create a theory of four bodily humors that determine human health and personality.

**1400 A.D.**—"Frenzy," a condition which includes overactive behavior, is treated by blood-letting, drugs, or shock treatment.

**1602 –1614**—Dr. Felix Platter of Switzerland advocates physical, psychological, and drug therapy for mental illness.

**1630**—French philosopher René Descartes suggests that the origin of mental problems lay in the brain.

**1820's**—Laws are passed in the United States to educate people with disabilities.

**1845**—Dr. Heinrich Hoffman, a German doctor, publishes the story of Fidgety Philip, the first appearance of a case of ADHD in print.

**1900**—Dr. Sigmund Freud teaches that behavior is influenced by childhood experiences, especially in the family environment.

**1902**—The English doctor Dr. George Still identifies "volitional inhibition," an inability to control actions in children. He feels its cause lay in the brain.

**1917 –1918**—An encephalitis outbreak causes doctors to use the name "brain-injured child syndrome" to describe all hyperactive children.

1937—Dr. William Bradley in Rhode Island gives Benzedrine to children after surgical procedures and discovers that it helps them to concentrate and act calmly.

1950s—The diagnostic term for hyperactive and inattentive behavior is changed to "minimal brain dysfunction" when it becomes apparent that children can be restless and hyperactive without brain damage.

1961—The medication Ritalin is approved by the Food and Drug Administration for treating children with hyperactivity.

1965—The American Psychiatric Association (APA) creates the first official diagnostic category for hyperactive and restless behavior: Hyperkinetic Reaction of Childhood.

1972—Dr. Virginia Douglas' research in Canada suggests that the cause of hyperactivity is a lack of impulse control and inattention.

1973—The Rehabilitation Act is passed, prohibiting discrimination on the basis of handicap for institutions that receive federal funds.

1975—U.S. Congress passes the Education for All Handicapped Children Act, which assures a free, appropriate public education for all children with disabilities.

1980—The APA splits the diagnostic category of Hyperkinetic Reaction of Childhood into two parts: Attention Deficit Disorder and Attention Deficit Disorder with Hyperactivity.

**1987**—The APA modifies the diagnostic categories to Undifferentiated Attention Deficit Disorder and Attention Deficit/Hyperactivity Disorder.

**1990**—The Americans with Disabilities Act is passed, prohibiting discrimination against people with disabilities in a wide range of situations.

**1991**—The Department of Education adds ADHD as a potentially disabling condition for the purposes of special education.

**1994**—The APA revises the categories a third time, back to one category, Attention-Deficit/Hyperactivity Disorder, and three subtypes: primarily inattentive, primarily hyperactive, and combined inattentive and hyperactive.

# Glossary

**ADA**—The Americans with Disabilities Act ensures fair treatment for workers with disabilities, including ADHD.

**ADD**—Attention Deficit Disorder, an older name for ADHD, still frequently used.

**ADD-H**—Attention Deficit Disorder with Hyperactivity, an older name for Attention Deficit with hyperactivity.

**ADHD**—Attention-Deficit/Hyperactivity Disorder, the term used since 1994 for this disorder.

**behavioral disinhibition**—The inability to plan, control, and regulate one's own behavior.

**biofeedback**—A technique used to regulate involuntary functions of the body, such as muscle tone, heart rate, and brain waves, to promote relaxation and calmness.

**cognitive therapy**—A psychological treatment that helps people express feelings in language rather than through inappropriate actions in their daily lives.

**corpus callosum**—A bridge of nerve cells connecting the two sides of the brain.

**developmental delay**—An interruption in a child's expected growth pattern.

**dopamine**—A neurotransmitter that helps the brain pay attention.

**DSM**—The Diagnostic and Statistical Manual of Mental Disorders, now in its fourth edition.

**encephalitis**—An inflammation of the brain.

**endorphins**—Chemicals in the brain that promote feelings of calmness and happiness.

**environment**—A person's external surroundings. This term is also used to cover any outside influence on a person, including behavioral or psychological therapy.

**fMRI**—Functional magnetic resonance imaging; computer-created pictures of parts of the body, including the brain, while they are working.

**hyperactivity**—Excessive, inappropriate physical motion or activity.

**IDEA**—Individuals with Disabilities Education Act, revised in 1997. IDEA sets up rules for special education programs and makes federal funds available for special education.

**IEP**—Individualized Education Program, written for students who qualify for special education under IDEA.

**IFSP**—Individualized Family Service Plan, an education and intervention plan for preschool children.

**impulsive**—Acting without thinking of the consequences.

**inattentive**—Not paying attention to what is important in a situation.

**MRI**—Magnetic resonance imaging; a computer-created picture of soft tissues using magnets to create the images.

**neurotransmitter**—The name given to several chemicals in the brain that help information pass from brain cell to brain cell.

**norepinephrine**—A neurotransmitter that helps the brain pay attention.

**perseveration**—Continuing to do an action that is inappropriate or not successful.

**PET**—Positron emission tomography; a computer-created picture of soft tissues in the body that requires radioactive material to make the picture.

**Section 504**—This section of the Rehabilitation Act of 1973 prohibits discrimination on the basis of handicap for institutions that receive federal funds.

**serotonin**—A neurotransmitter associated with attention and depression.

**SSRI**—Selective serotonin reuptake inhibitors; a type of antidepressant medication that keep the level of serotonin high in the brain.

**stimulant medication**—Drugs that increase the level of dopamine and norepinephrine in the brain.

**tics**—Involuntary muscle spasms.

# For More Information

**Children and Adults with Attention Deficit Disorder (CHADD)**
8181 Professional Place, Suite 201
Landover, MD 20785
(800) 233-4050
(301) 306-7070

**The Council for Exceptional Children**
1920 Association Drive
Reston, VA 20191-1589
(888) CEC-SPED
(703) 620-3660

**National Attention Deficit Disorder Association (ADDA)**
1788 Second Street, Suite 200
Highland Park, IL 60035
(847) 432-ADDA

**National Institute of Mental Health**
6001 Executive Boulevard, Room 8184, MSC 9663
Bethesda, MD 20892-9663
(301) 443-4513

**United States Department of Education**
400 Maryland Avenue, SW
Washington, D.C. 20202-0498
(800) USA-LEARN

# Chapter Notes

## Chapter 1. Not Just a Bratty Kid

1. Margaret Cousins, *The Story of Thomas Alva Edison* (New York: Random House, 1965), pp. 12–13, 46, 71–75.

2. Russell A. Barkley, *ADHD: The Complete, Authoritative Guide for Parents* (New York: Guilford Press, 1995), p. 3.

3. Lawrence H. Diller, *Running on Ritalin* (New York: Bantam Books, 1998), p. 2.

4. Daniel Seligman, *A Question of Intelligence* (New York: Carol Publishing Group, 1992), pp. 41–43.

5. David B. Stein, *Ritalin Is Not the Answer* (San Francisco: Jossey-Bass Publishers, 1999), p. xv.

6. Joseph Biederman, "Pro and Con: Are Stimulants Overprescribed for Children with Behavioral Problems?" *Pediatric News,* August 1996, p. 26.

7. American Psychiatric Association, *Diagnostic and Statistical Manual of Mental Disorders,* Fourth Edition (Washington, D.C.: American Psychiatric Association, 1994), p. 85.

8. Diller, pp. 315–317.

## Chapter 2. What Is ADHD?

1. Marianne Mercugliano, et al., *The Clinician's Practical Guide to Attention-Deficit/Hyperactivity Disorder* (Baltimore, Md: Paul H. Brooks Publishing Co., 1999), p. 2.

2. Michael W. Cohen, *The Attention Zone: A Parent's Guide to Attention Deficit/Hyperactivity Disorder* (Washington, D.C.: Brunner/Mazel, 1998), p. 9.

3. Ibid., pp. 12–13.

4. Russell A. Barkley, *ADHD: The Complete, Authoritative Guide for Parents* (New York: Guilford Press, 1995), p. 55.

5. Phyllis Anne Teeter, *Interventions for ADHD: Treatment in Developmental Context* (New York: Guilford Press, 1998), pp. 2–3.

6. Mercugliano, p. xi.

7. Teeter, p. 3.

8. Barkley, p. 3.

9. Joseph Biederman, "Pro and Con: Are Stimulants Overprescribed for Children with Behavioral Problems?" *Pediatric News,* August 1996, p. 26.

10. Mercugliano, p.5.

11. Lawrence H. Diller, *Running on Ritalin* (New York: Bantam Books, 1998), pp. 35–36.

12. Edna D. Copeland and Valerie L. Love, *Attention Without Tension—A Teacher's Handbook on Attention Disorders, ADHD and ADD* (Plantation, Fla.: Specialty Press, Inc., 1995), p. 4.

13. Mercugliano, p. 9.

14. Alan J. Zametkin, et al., "Cerebral Glucose Metabolism in Adults with Hyperactivity of Childhood Onset," *New England Journal of Medicine,* November 15, 1990, pp. 1361–1366.

15. Alan J. Zametkin, et al., "Brain Metabolism in Teenagers with Attention-Deficit Hyperactivity Disorder," *Archives of General Psychiatry,* May 1993, pp. 333–340.

16. P. Nopoulos, et al., "Developmental Brain Anomalies in Children with Attention-Deficit Hyperactivity Disorder," *Journal of Child Neurology,* February 2000, pp. 102–108.

17. Michael I. Posner and Marcus E. Raichle, *Images of Mind* (New York: Scientific American Library, 1994), p. 224.

18. Barkley, p. 64.

19. Teeter, p. 85.

20. Ibid., pp. 170–171.

21. Ibid., p. 319.

## Chapter 3. The History of ADHD

1. Roy Porter, *The Greatest Benefit to Mankind: A Medical History of Humanity* (New York: W.W. Norton and Co., 1997), p. 58.

2. Lawrence H. Diller, *Running on Ritalin* (New York: Bantam Books, 1998), p. 9.

3. Simon Hornblower and Anthony Spawforth, ed., *The Oxford Classical Dictionary*, Third Edition, (Oxford, England: Oxford University Press, 1996), p. 947.

4. Porter, pp. 127–128.

5. Logan Clendening, *Source Book of Medical History* (New York: Dover Publications, 1942), p. 87.

6. Porter, pp. 196–197.

7. Lois N. Magner, *A History of Medicine* (New York: Marcel Dekker, 1992), p. 111.

8. Porter, pp. 242–243.

9. Oscar Papazian, "The Story of Fidgety Philip," *International Pediatrics*, Vol. 10, No. 2, 1995, pp. 188–190.

10. American Psychiatric Association, *Diagnostic and Statistical Manual of Mental Disorders, Second Edition* (Washington, D.C.: American Psychiatric Association, 1965).

11. Diller, p. 53.

12. Mortimer D. Gross, "Origin of Stimulant Use for Treatment of Attention Deficit Disorder," *American Journal of Psychiatry*, Volume 152, February 1995, pp. 298–299.

13. Charles Bradley, "The Behavior of Children Receiving Benzedrine," *American Journal of Psychiatry*, Volume 94, 1937, pp. 577–585.

## Chapter 4. Identifying ADHD in Children and Adults

1. H. Rutherford Turnbull III and Ann P. Turnbull, *Free Appropriate Public Education, Sixth Edition* (Denver, Colo.: Love Publishing Co., 2000), p. 139.

2. Phyllis Anne Teeter, *Interventions for ADHD: Treatment in Developmental Context* (New York: Guilford Press, 1998), pp. 21 and 74.

3. Ibid., p. 97.

4. Marianne Mercugliano, et al., *The Clinician's Practical Guide to Attention-Deficit/Hyperactivity Disorder* (Baltimore, Md: Paul H. Brooks Publishing Co., 1999), p. 81.

5. Ibid., pp. 27–30.

6. S. Buttross, "Attention Deficit-Hyperactivity Disorder and Its Deceivers," *Current Problems in Pediatrics,* February 30, 2000, pp. 37–50.

7. Steven R. Pliszka, et al., *ADHD With Comorbid Disorders* (New York: Guilford Press, 1999), p. 5.

8. Teeter, p. 105.

9. Pliszka, pp. 9–11.

10. American Academy of Pediatrics, "Practice Guideline," *Pediatrics,* Vol. 105, No. 5, May 2000, p. 1164.

11. E.M. Mitsis, et al., "Parent-teacher Concordance for DSM-IV Attention-Deficit/Hyperactivity Disorder in a Clinic-Referred Sample," *Journal of the American Academy of Child and Adolescent Psychiatry,* March 2000, pp. 308–313.

12. American Psychiatric Association, *Diagnostic and Statistical Manual of Mental Disorders, Fourth Edition* (Washington, D.C.: American Psychiatric Association, 1994), pp. 83–85.

13. American Academy of Pediatrics, pp. 1158–1170.

14. Paul H. Wender, *Attention-Deficit Hyperactivity Disorder in Adults* (New York: Oxford University Press, 1995), pp. 241–247.

## Chapter 5. Treating ADHD

1. Michael W. Cohen, *The Attention Zone: A Parent's Guide to Attention Deficit/Hyperactivity Disorder* (Washington, D.C.: Brunner/Mazel, 1998), p. 65.

2. Phyllis Anne Teeter, *Interventions for ADHD: Treatment in Developmental Context* (New York: Guilford Press, 1998), p. 150.

3. Ibid., pp. 152–154.

4. Edna D. Copeland and Valerie L. Love, *Attention Without Tension—A Teacher's Handbook on Attention Disorders, ADHD and ADD* (Plantation, Fla.: Specialty Press, Inc., 1995), p. 88.

5. David B. Stein, *Ritalin Is Not The Answer* (San Francisco: Jossey-Bass Publishers, 1999), p. 78.

6. Cohen, pp. 119–121.

7. Ben F. Feingold, *Why Your Child Is Hyperactive* (New York: Random House, 1974), pp. 30–43.

8. Diana Hunter, *The Ritalin-Free Child: Managing Hyperactivity and Attention Deficits Without Drugs,* (Ft. Lauderdale, Fla.: Consumer Press, 1995), p. 63.

9. Selene Yeager, et al., *Prevention's New Foods for Healing* (Emmaus, Pa: Rodale Press, Inc., 1998), pp. 177, 180, 196, 569.

10. Rhoda Fukushima, "Karate Kids: Program Helps ADD Children Focus," *The Press Democrat,* sec. D, pp. 1–2, August 1, 2000.

11. Mary Ann Block, "Attention on Kids," *Energy Times,* September 2000, pp. 43–47.

12. Cohen, pp. 142–144.

13. Ibid., pp. 153–158.

14. National Institute of Mental Health, "Collaborative Study Finds Effective Treatments for ADHD," Press Release, December 14, 1999 <http://www.nimh.nih.gov/events/prmta.cfm>. (March 2001).

15. Nicole Ziegler Dizon, "Teens Might Be Using Ritalin For Recreation," *Morning Call,* sec. A, p. 20, April 7, 2000.

16. Teeter, pp. 247–248.

17. Russell A. Barkley, *ADHD: The Complete, Authoritative Guide for Parents* (New York: Guilford Press, 1995), p. 249.

18. Julie Magno Zito, et al.,"Trends in the Prescribing of Psychotropic Medications for Preschoolers," *Journal of the American Medical Association,* February 23, 2000, pp. 1025–1030.

19. Marianne Mercugliano, et al., *The Clinician's Practical Guide to Attention-Deficit/Hyperactivity Disorder* (Baltimore, Md: Paul H. Brooks Publishing Co., 1999), p. 205.

20. National Institutes of Health News Advisory, "Ensuring Safe and Effective Psychotropic Medications for Children," April 23, 1999 <http://www.nimh.nih.gov/events/prkidsmeds.cfm> (March 2001).

21. Teeter, p. 245.

## Chapter 6. Strategies for Success in School

1. United States Department of Education, memorandum from the assistant secretary of the Office of Special Education and Rehabilitative Service, September 16, 1991 <http://www.add.org/content/legal/memo.htm> (May 2001).

2. H. Rutherford Turnbull III and Ann P. Turnbull, *Free Appropriate Public Education, Sixth Edition* (Denver, Colo.: Love Publishing Co., 2000), p. 15.

3. United States Department of Education memorandum.

4. Lawrence H. Diller, *Running on Ritalin* (New York: Bantam Books, 1998), pp. 148–149.

5. IDEA '97 Final Regulations, *Federal Register,* March 12, 1999, Section 1, Title I and II, parts 300–304.

6. Turnbull, pp. 143–144.

7. Diana Hunter, *The Ritalin-Free Child: Managing Hyperactivity and Attention Deficits Without Drugs* (Ft. Lauderdale, Fla.: Consumer Press, 1995), pp. 86–92.

8. Michael W. Cohen, *The Attention Zone: A Parent's Guide to Attention Deficit/Hyperactivity Disorder* (Washington, D.C.: Brunner/Mazel, 1998), pp. 103–104.

9. Brigitte Greenberg, "Disabled Going To College," *Morning Call,* sec. A, p. 4, February 10, 2000.

10. Patricia O. Quinn, *Attention Deficit Disorder: Diagnosis and Treatment from Infancy to Adulthood* (New York: Brunner/Mazel, 1997), p. 130.

11. Ibid., p. 131.

## Chapter 7. ADHD and Society

1. Phyllis Anne Teeter, *Interventions for ADHD: Treatment in Developmental Context* (New York: Guilford Press, 1998), p. 283.

2. Lawrence H. Diller, *Running on Ritalin* (New York: Bantam Books, 1998), p. 279.

3. A. D. Sandler, "Attention Deficits and Neurodevelopmental Variation in Older Adolescents and Adults," in K.G. Nadeau (Ed.), *A Comprehensive Guide to Attention-Deficit Disorder in Adults: Research, Diagnosis, and Treatment* (New York: Brunner/Mazel, 1995), p. 66.

4. Julie K.L. Dam and Samantha Miller, "The Family Still Matters," *People Magazine,* December 13, 1999, p. 79.

5. Teeter, p. 288.

6. Diller, pp. 164–166.

7. Teeter, pp. 135–141.

8. Ibid., pp. 314–319.

9. Ibid., p. 311.

10. Diller, pp. 307–308.

11. Julia Lawlor, "No Panic. No Shame. Just Doing a Job," *New York Times,* sec. G, p. 1, June 14, 2000.

12. Tara Parker-Pope, "Drug Firms Research Behavioral Therapies That Last a School Day," *The Wall Street Journal,* sec. B, p. 1, May 12, 2000.

## Chapter 8. The Future and ADHD

1. Phyllis Anne Teeter, *Interventions for ADHD: Treatment in Developmental Context* (New York: Guilford Press, 1998), pp. 320–321.

2. A.E. Kayle, et al., "Quantitative Morphology of the Corpus Callosum in Children with Neurofibromatosis and Attention-Deficit Hyperactivity Disorder," *Journal of Child Neurology,* February 2000, pp. 90–96.

3. Teeter, pp. 322–323.

4. Anton Van Dellen, et al., "Delaying the Onset of Huntington's in Mice," *Nature,* April 13, 2000, pp. 721–722.

5. E. A. Maguire, et al., "Navigation-related Structural Change in the Hippocampi of Taxi Drivers," *Proceedings of the National Academy of Sciences of the United States of America,* April 11, 2000, pp. 4398–4403.

6. National Institutes of Health, "Consensus Development Conference Statement: Diagnosis and Treatment of Attention-Deficit/Hyperactivity Disorder," *Journal of the American Academy of Child and Adolescent Psychiatry,* February 2000, pp. 182–193.

7. David B. Stein, *Ritalin Is Not The Answer* (San Francisco: Jossey-Bass Publishers, 1999), pp. 9 and 22.

8. Thomas Armstrong, *The Myth of the ADD Child* (New York: Dutton, 1995), p. 8.

9. Lawrence H. Diller, *Running on Ritalin* (New York: Bantam Books, 1998), pp. 315–318.

10. Eben Carle, "ADHD for Sale," *Psychology Today,* June 2000, p. 17.

11. Diller, p. 331. This view has also been expressed by Jason Sholl in his review article, "Dangerous Distraction," *Reason,* May 2000, pp. 52–55.

12. Russell A. Barkley, *ADHD: The Complete, Authoritative Guide for Parents* (New York: Guilford Press, 1995), p. 253.

13. India Knight, "Perfectly Mad Parenting," *London Times,* April 16, 2000, News Review, p. 3.

14. IMS Health press release, September 11, 1998 <http://www.imshealth.com/html/news_arc/09_11_1998_101.htm> (March 2001).

15. K. Hoagwood, et al., "Treatment Services for Children with ADHD: A National Perspective," *Journal of the American Academy of Child and Adolescent Psychiatry,* February 2000, pp. 198–206.

16. Barkley, p. 65; Diller, p. 50.

17. Thom Hartmann, *Beyond ADD: Hunting for Reasons in the Past and Present* (Grass Valley, Calif.: Underwood Books, 1996), p. xv.

18. Elizabeth Russell Connelly, *Conduct Unbecoming* (Philadelphia: Chelsea House Publishing, 1999), p. 91.

# Further Reading

## Books

Dolber, Roslyn. *College and Career Success for Students with Learning Disabilities.* Lincolnwood, Ill.: NTC/Contemporary Publishing Co., 1996.

Dwyer, Kathleen. *What Do You Mean I Have Attention Deficit Disorder?* New York: Walker, 1996.

Gordon, Michael. *My Brother's A World-Class Pain; A Sibling's Guide to ADHD—Hyperactivity.* DeWitt, NY: GSI Publications, 1992.

McCutcheon, Randall J. *Get Off My Brain—A Survival Guide for Lazy\* Students (\*Bored, Frustrated, and Otherwise Sick of School).* Minneapolis, Minn.: Free Spirit Publishing, 1998.

Nadeau, Kathleen, and Ellen Dixon. *Learning to Slow Down and Pay Attention: A Book for Kids about ADD, second ed.* Washington, D.C.: Magination Press, 1997.

Quinn, Patricia. *ADD and the College Student: A Guide for High School and College Students with Attention Deficit Disorder. Revised ed.* Washington, D.C.: Magination Press, 2001.

Romain, Trevoraut. *How to Do Homework Without Throwing Up.* Minneapolis, Minn.: Free Spirit Publishing, 1997.

Sirotowitz, Sandi. *Study Strategies Made Easy; A Practical Plan for School Success.* Plantation, Fla.: Specialty Press, Inc., 1996. (Also has a video.)

Weaver, Constance, ed. *Success at Last!: Helping Students with AD(H)D Achieve Their Potential.* Portsmouth, N.H.: Heinemann, 1994.

## Articles

Adesman, Andrew, M.D. "Does My Child Need Ritalin?" *Newsweek*, April 24, 2000, p. 81.

"Attention Please!" *Vegetarian Times,* September 1, 1999, pp. 68–75. (A nutrition-based approach to treating ADHD.)

Brush, Stephanie. "Can't Concentrate: Feeling Fidgety? Utterly Overwhelmed?" *Mademoiselle,* February 1, 2000, pp. 116–119.

Gibbs, Nancy. "The Age of Ritalin." *Time,* November 30, 1998, pp. 86–96. (Other related articles appear in this edition.)

Rodgers, Kathleen M. "Profiles in Love: Driven to Distraction." *Family Circle,* October 6, 1998, pp. 144–149.

Vatz, Richard E. "How Accurate is Media Coverage of Attention Deficit Disorder?" *USA Today,* July 1, 1997, pp. 76–77.

## Film and Video

*Adults with Attention Deficit Disorder—ADD Isn't Just Kids Stuff.* Glen Elyn, Ill.: Child Management, Inc., 1994.

*Differences.* Skokie, Ill.: Rush Neurobehavioral Center, 1999.

*It's Just Attention Disorder—A Video for Kids.* King of Prussia, Pa.: Childswork/Childsplay, 1992.

# Internet Addresses

ADDitude, a lifestyle magazine for people with ADHD
<http://www.additudemag.com>

ADHDNews.com, an online newsletter with up-to-the-minute news, reviews, and research for parents
<http://www.adhdnews.com>

Born to Explore: the other side of ADHD
<http://www.borntoexplore.org>

Children and Adults with Attention-Deficit/Hyperactivity Disorder
<http://www.chadd.org>

National Attention Deficit Disorder Association
<http://www.add.org>

# Index